ANTHROPOLOGICAL PAPERS

MUSEUM OF ANTHROPOLOGY, UNIVERSITY OF MICHIGAN

NO. 40

EARLY PUEBLOAN OCCUPATIONS AT TESUQUE BY-PASS AND IN THE UPPER RIO GRANDE VALLEY

BY

CHARLES H. MCNUTT

APPENDIX BY

ARTHUR J. JELINEK

ANN ARBOR

THE UNIVERSITY OF MICHIGAN, 1969

ISBN (print): 978-0-932206-38-1
ISBN (ebook): 978-1-951519-30-8

Browse all of our books at
sites.lsa.umich.edu/archaeology-books.

Order our books from the University of Michigan
Press at www.press.umich.edu.

For permissions, questions, or manuscript queries,
contact Museum publications by email at umma-pubs@umich.edu or visit the Museum website at
lsa.umich.edu/ummaa.

TABLE OF CONTENTS

TABLE OF CONTENTS

LIST OF FIGURES

[illegible]

11. Distribution in the Rio Grande Valley [illegible]
Pottery Types [illegible]

12. Distribution in the Rio Grande Valley of Santa [illegible]
Pottery Types [illegible]

13. Maximum Distribution of [illegible]
[illegible]

LIST OF PLATES

(Follow page 133)

[illegible]

[illegible]

[illegible]

[illegible]

[illegible]

[illegible]

[illegible]

[illegible]

[illegible]

[illegible]

X. Excavation Photographs, Area [illegible]

XI. Excavation Photographs, Area B

FORWARD

THIS monograph is a slightly revised version of a dissertation submitted to the University of Michigan in 1959. In preparing it for publication, no attempt has been made to bring the report up-to-date. The primary reason for this is my nonparticipation in archeology of the southwestern United States since writing the original report. There are many others whose qualifications to incorporate current research into this study are far superior. Much of the "current research" mentioned in the concluding section has been completed and some of the results have been published. Such of the latter as has come to my attention does not, in my opinion, call for any major revision of the hypotheses presented. Certain changes in emphasis and definition of distributional boundaries are in order, and footnotes are inserted at the appropriate places in the text. The descriptive data, of course, retain their original significance.

I would like to express my very sincere gratitude to Dr. James B. Griffin of the Museum of Anthropology, University of Michigan, who not only served as chairman of the dissertation committee but also provided invaluable assistance in the preparation of this monograph.

Charles H. McNutt, 1968

PREFACE

THE New Mexico Highway Salvage Archaeological Program is a cooperative project of the New Mexico State Highway Department, the Bureau of Public Roads, the Department of the Interior, and the Museum of New Mexico. It has preserved a great amount of data from a major section of the southwestern United States and provided a model for a new and important phase of prehistoric research. Many individuals from many professions have contributed to this project, but Dr. Fred Wendorf and Mr. Stewart Peckham must be given particular credit as the original and present program directors, respectively.

The New Mexico project is particularly fortunate in that it has available the extensive site surveys, collections, and site maps of the Laboratory of Anthropology (Museum of New Mexico), the greatest parts of which are the work of Dr. H. P. Mera and Mr. Stanley A. Stubbs. This does not, of course, preclude the necessity for an additional survey of each new highway right-of-way. It does, however, greatly facilitate this task and frequently saves considerable time in situations in which time is a vital factor.

The site with which this report is concerned is recorded in the files of the Laboratory of Anthropology as L.A. 3294. (L.A. stands for Laboratory of Anthropology; site numbers are assigned serially and have no spatial significance.) It was discovered during the survey of a highway project designed to by-pass the town (not the pueblo) of Tesuque, New Mexico, north of Santa Fe. Because plans of the New Mexico State Highway Department called for removal of most of the sand and gravel ridge upon which L.A. 3294 was located, investigation of the site was included in the New Mexico Highway Salvage Archaeology program. I was in charge of excavations at this site, which were conducted from June 21 through July 31, 1955.

The problems arising from these excavations and treated in this study are five in number. In starkest outline, they are: (1) to present the data obtained from the excavations; (2) to analyze evidences of human occupancy at the site; (3) to interpret such evidences by relating them to data from other occupations in the immediate and adjacent areas; (4) to formulate that general interpretation of prehistoric occupations in the area which is in closest accord with such information as is available; (5) to isolate subjects for future research which will be most pertinent to a more complete understanding of local prehistory.

Three distinctive occupations, or cultural components, were found at the Tesuque By-Pass Site. Each represents a stage of the early (pre-classic) Puebloan occupation in the Santa Fe-Tesuque portion of the upper Rio Grande Valley.[1] These are both described and analyzed in Part One of this report.

An interpretation of these occupations and the determination of their relationships to other cultural manifestations in adjacent areas are presented in Part Two. Certain conclusions either supplement or suggest alternatives to current interpretations of the local prehistoric culture-sequence.

In the third and final section of this report these data are summarized, an interpretation of upper Rio Grande Valley prehistory is presented, and particularly vital subjects for future research are suggested.

I should like to express my appreciation to the New Mexico State Highway Department for providing labor for the excavation, to Dr. Fred Wendorf for his helpful supervision, and to Mr. Stewart Peckham for the time, effort, and additional information which he has contributed. To Stanley Stubbs, who has ever placed his unequalled knowledge of the area at the disposal of interested students, I am indebted for discussions and ideas which have proved invaluable. Mr. Arthur J. Jelinek has added to this report one of the few extant discussions of mammalian fauna of the early Puebloan period, and his contribution will be welcomed by many. A number of individuals, in addition to those whom I have mentioned,

1 "Puebloan" is used in this discussion as a very general reference to the pottery-making people characteristic of the prehistoric period in eastern Arizona, western New Mexico, and adjacent portions of Utah and Colorado to the north. This usage corresponds roughly to Reed's (1942) use of the term. The "upper Rio Grande Valley" refers to that portion of the valley extending from the vicinity of Isleta Pueblo in the south to the New Mexico – Colorado State boundary in the north, following the definitions of Wendorf (1954) and Wendorf and Reed (1955).

contributed their knowledge and ideas. At the risk of overlooking the many to specify the few, particular thanks are due Mr. Jerry Dawson (University of New Mexico), Dr. A. E. Dittert, Jr. (Laboratory of Anthropology), Mr. Bruce Ellis (Museum of New Mexico), and Dr. Florence Ellis (University of New Mexico).

Dr. James B. Griffin of the Museum of Anthropology, University of Michigan made my own participation in this project possible, obtained laboratory space for the artifact analysis, and was a constant source of encouragement for my efforts.

Finally, I must add that I am one of those most fortunate of archeologists: my wife, Phoebe, can typewrite.

Charles H. McNutt, 1959

I

THE TESUQUE BY-PASS SITE

(L.A. 3294)

INTRODUCTION

THE Tesuque By-Pass Site is located in Santa Fe County, New Mexico, SE¼ NE¼ Sec. 23 and SW¼ Sec. 24, T 18 N, R 9 E. It is approximately 1.25 miles northwest of the town (not pueblo) of Tesuque. The site is located on a high sand and gravel ridge which forms the western boundary of the Rio Tesuque, an intermittent stream which joins the Rio Nambe (or Pojoaque) and empties into the Rio Grande.

The site (Fig. 1) is reached by crossing the usually dry bed of Rio Tesuque and climbing a steep grade up the end of a narrow ridge. The grade begins to level off approximately 55 ft. above the bottom of the river bed (elevation of the river bed here is 6,565 ft. above mean sea level [m.s.l.]). Continuing in an upstream direction (southeast), the crest of the ridge rises gradually. Surface indications of the site are first encountered about 100 ft. from the northwest end of the ridge. At this point, the habitable portion of the ridgetop is about 90 ft. wide. To the northeast, the ridge drops almost vertically, having been eroded and undercut by past water action of the Rio Tesuque.

The site is marked by bits of pottery, occasional points, flakes of stone, and alignments of vertical stone slabs representing the foundations of old walls. These remains were found for about 200 yds. along the top of the ridge.

The site is situated in the broken country between the foothills of the Sangre de Cristos and the Rio Grande, where typical Upper Sonoran flora prevails. Vegetation is sparse, especially on the ridge and hilltops, and consists of sagebrush, grama grass, juniper, and cacti. Cottonwood trees are found occasionally along the edge of Rio Tesuque, becoming more numerous as one proceeds downstream.

METHODS OF EXCAVATION

Indications of human occupancy are not distributed uniformly

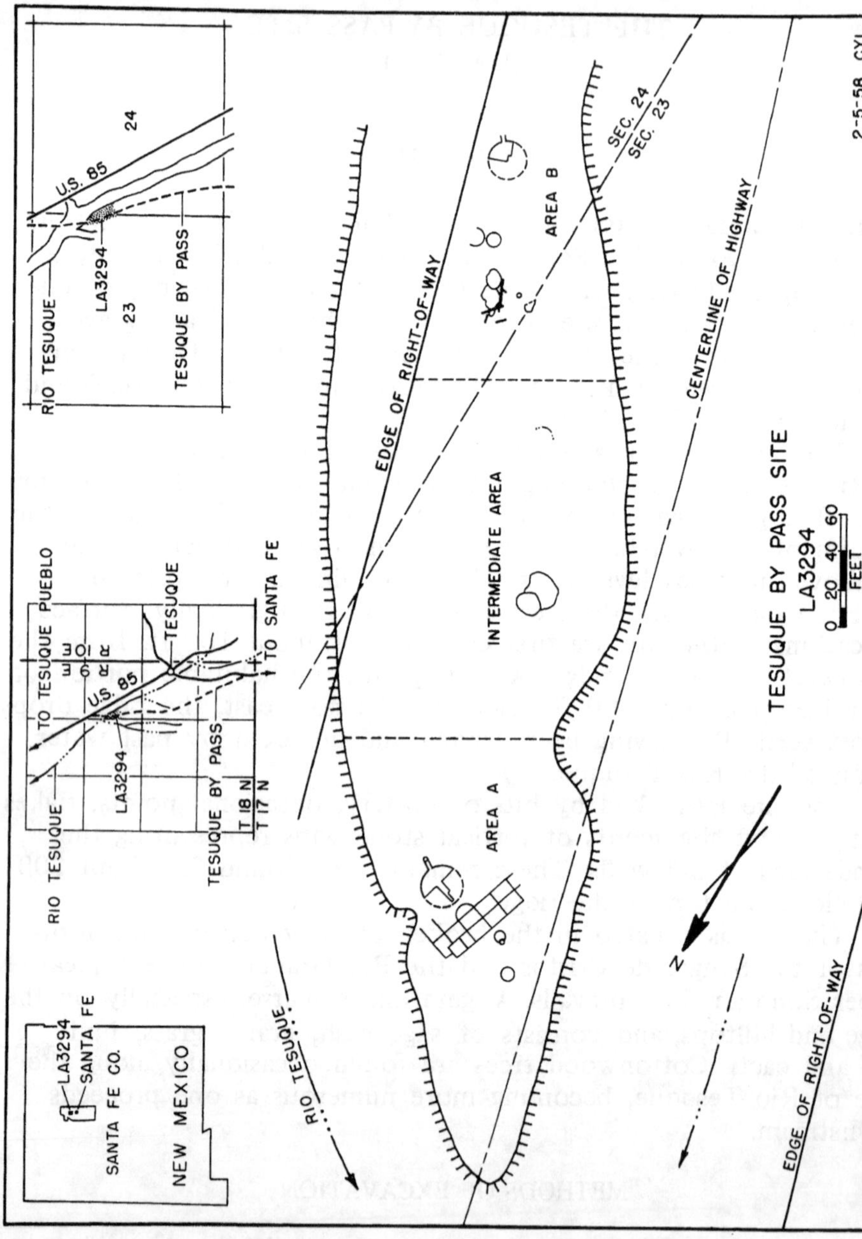
TESUQUE BY PASS SITE
LA3294
0 20 40 60
FEET
2-5-58 C.Y.L.
RIO TESUQUE
LA3294
23
TESUQUE BY PASS
U.S. 85
24
RIO TESUQUE
TO TESUQUE PUEBLO
TESUQUE
U.S. 85
LA3294
TESUQUE BY PASS
T 18 N
T 17 N
TO SANTA FE
9 E
R
LA3294
SANTA FE
SANTA FE CO.
NEW MEXICO
EDGE OF RIGHT-OF-WAY
SEC. 24
SEC. 23
AREA B
INTERMEDIATE AREA
AREA A
CENTERLINE OF HIGHWAY
RIO TESUQUE
EDGE OF RIGHT-OF-WAY
N

Figure 1

over the surface of the Tesuque By-Pass Site. Two areas of artifact concentration were noted about 475 ft. apart. Surface collections indicated that Kwahe'e B/W sherds occurred more frequently than other types of painted pottery in the area nearest the northwest (downstream) end of the ridge. In the other area, Santa Fe B/W appeared predominant. As testing proceeded, certain finds were made in the central portion of the site which could not be attributed to either of the major areas. Hence, the site was divided into three areas: "Area A" was used to designate the concentration of remains associated with the Kwahe'e B/W; "Area B" was used to designate the concentration of remains associated with Santa Fe B/W; the intermediate area was designated as such.

Test pits were dug throughout the site. Usually, sterile soil was encountered within 6 to 8 in. below the surface. In other places, excavation continued until sterile soil was reached. These pits were then enlarged to investigate the various features.

Room floors were found less than a foot below the surface. The only extensive use of stratigraphic control was in the excavation of the kiva in Area A, where a considerable depth of fill and quantity of cultural material were found. In this feature, four stratigraphically distinct levels were distinguished, designated I–IV from top to bottom. In other cases, finds from the fill were separated from those encountered within 3 to 4 in. above floor level.

After five and one-half weeks of excavation, I made my final notes and maps and left the Santa Fe area for a brief period, during which time Mr. Stewart Peckham of the Laboratory of Anthropology engaged in additional excavation at the site. His information has added greatly to the results of this project.

(AREA A)

ARCHITECTURE

The remains of an L-shaped room-block, a circular kiva, and four exterior pits were found (Fig. 2). The longer section of the room-block is composed of eight rooms, arranged in pairs along a north-south axis. The greater dimension of the floors is parallel to this axis. At the southern end of this section, a single room extends southward from the eastern row of rooms. It was not completely excavated.

The base of the "L" is formed by what is probably two rooms, placed end to end. These rooms join the line of paired rooms at its northern end and extend eastward almost to the edge

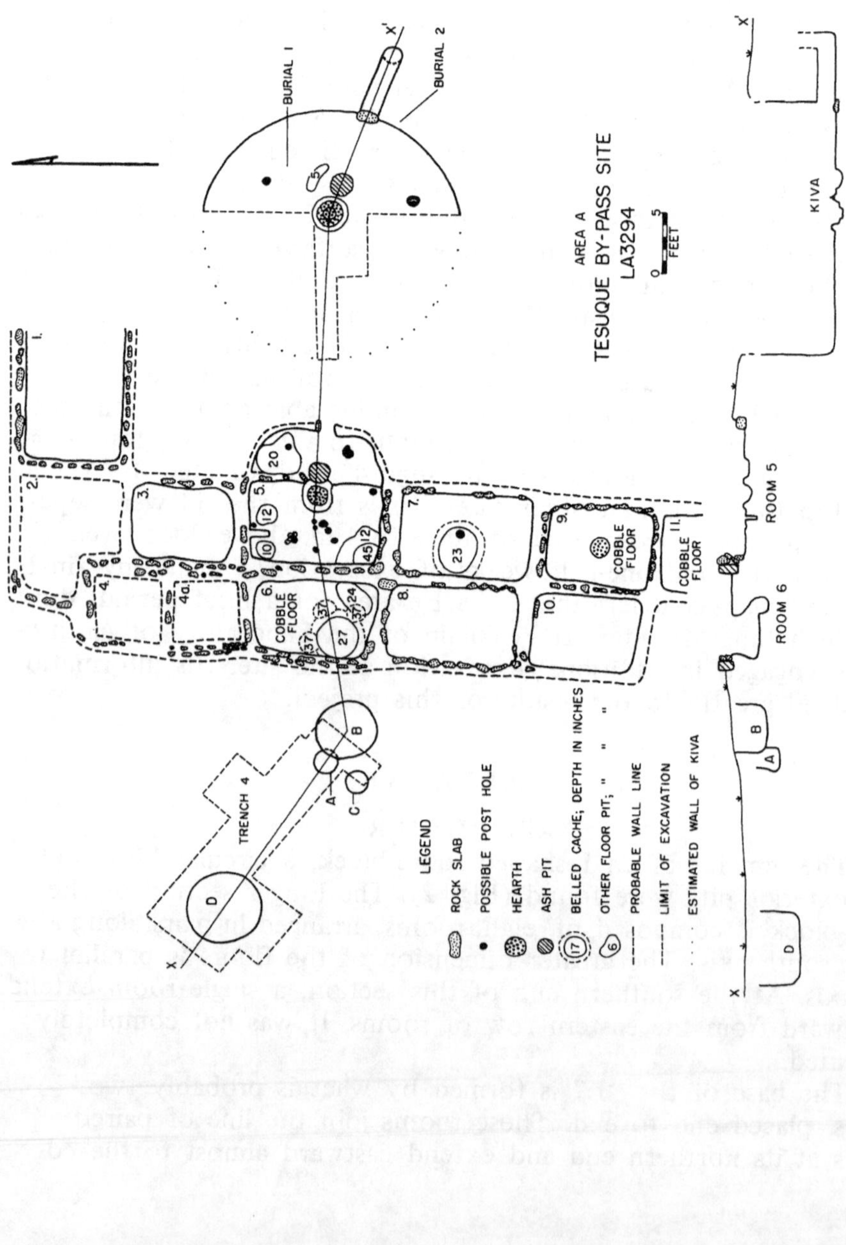
AREA A
TESUQUE BY-PASS SITE
LA3294
0 5
FEET
LEGEND
ROCK SLAB
POSSIBLE POST HOLE
HEARTH
ASH PIT
BELLED CACHE; DEPTH IN INCHES
OTHER FLOOR PIT; " " "
PROBABLE WALL LINE
LIMIT OF EXCAVATION
ESTIMATED WALL OF KIVA
BURIAL 1
BURIAL 2
TRENCH 4
COBBLE FLOOR
ROOM 6
ROOM 5
KIVA
X
X'

Figure 2

of the ridge. It is possible that this row of rooms may have extended farther to the east. If so, all traces of the extension have been removed by the erosion of a small wash which drains off the top of the bluff at this point. This wash also removed the eastern wall of room 1 (the northeastern extremity of the room-block).

The kiva is located within the right-angled area defined by the room-block. The pits are on the other side and apparently are placed randomly.

Rooms

Data from the various rooms are presented in Table 1. Three rooms have roughly cobbled floors (Nos. 6, 9, and 11). Other floors are of clay. Hearths were found in only two rooms (No. 4 and No. 9). One room (No. 7) appears to have a single central post. In most cases, wall foundations are of upright stone slabs set into adobe. Considerable variation in the use of the upright stone slabs occurs, especially in those walls common to two rooms. In some cases the slabs appear to function as a facing for an adobe wall, in other cases the slabs are used to form a stone core for the adobe walls. Floor-pits are common, especially in the western bank of rooms. Most of these pits are excavated into sterile soil and are unplastered.

Room No. 5 is of particular interest. At first, it appeared to be a rectangular room with a well-made hearth set into the middle of its east wall. Further excavation (by Peckham) disclosed a semicircular extension of the floor beyond the eastern wall. Evidently the room had been D-shaped at one time, rather than rectangular. This suggests that room No. 5 was once used for ceremonial purposes.

Kiva

A little more than half of the kiva in Area A was excavated (Pl. X, *b*). It is circular, diameter ca. 21 ft.

Walls: Unshaped stones, aligned in rough courses, set in copious amount of adobe. Wall thickness ca. 6 in., standing 5 ft. above floor. Plastered with 0.25 in. layer of clay. No reinforcing posts found in wall.

Floor: Thin layer of adobe clay (0.25 in.) over sterile sand and

TABLE 1

DIMENSIONS OF UNITS IN THE ROOM-BLOCK, AREA A

Room Number	Interior Length	Interior Width	Floor	Room Features		
				Hearth	Pit	Post
1	11 ft. 5 in.	8 ft. 5 in.	Clay	. . .	. . .	. . .
2	?	8 ft. 2 in.	Unex.	. . .	. . .	. . .
3	9 ft. 2 in.	7 ft. 2 in.	Unex.	. . .	. . .	. . .
4	10 ft. 11 in.	5 ft. 11 in.	Unex.	. . .	. . .	. . .
5	11 ft. 1 in.	7 ft. 5 in.	Clay	x	x	x
6	8 ft. 8 in.	5 ft. 10 in.	Cobble	. . .	. . .	. . .
7	11 ft.	6 ft. 10 in.	Clay	. . .	. . .	x
8	10 ft. 5 in.	6 ft. 1 in.	Clay	. . .	. . .	. . .
9	8 ft. 4 in.	6 ft. 2 in.	Cobble	x	. . .	. . .
10	7 ft. 5 in.	6 ft. 2 in.	Clay	. . .	. . .	. . .
11	?	6 ft. 2 in.	Cobble	. . .	. . .	. . .

Note – x designates presence of individual room features.

gravel. Average depth below sloping ground level 7 ft. 2 in.; minimum 6 ft. 8 in., maximum 7 ft. 7 in.

Hearth: Circular, clay-lined basin, located on axis passing from ventilator to rear wall through center of kiva; hearth center 8 ft. 6 in. from ventilator opening, ca. 12 ft. from rear wall. Encircled by clay coping 4 in. wide, 2 in. high. Small rock slabs (5 by 6 by 0.75 in.) set into coping along front of hearth, protruding to height of 5 in. above floor. Interior diameter of hearth 2 ft. 2 in., depth 4 in. Secondary depression in center of hearth 11 in. diameter, reaching depth of 6 in. below floor. Entire hearth filled with white ash.

Ashpit: Circular, clay-lined basin, located on same axis as hearth; center 5 ft. 6 in. from ventilator opening. Diameter 1 ft. 7 in., depth 8 in.; filled with white ash. No coping or other secondary features.

Ladder-post socket (?): Depressed area on (north) side of ashpit. Roughly oval with one long side slightly concave; long axis roughly parallel to hearth-ventilator axis. Length 2 ft. 6 in., width 9 in., depth 5 in. Interpretation tenuous.

Deflector or damper slab: Broken sandstone slab on floor near ventilator; originally 1 ft. 4 in. by 9 in. by 1.5 in. No deflector socket or support discovered.

Ventilator: Wall opening roughly circular, 1 ft. 5 in. diameter, with bottom at floor level. Ventilator tunnel turns upward at a point 5 ft. 8 in. behind wall. A small stone slab 1 ft. 2 in. by 8 in. by 2 in. is set in adobe on floor of ventilator tunnel, projecting 6 in. inside kiva wall-line. The adobe mortar, used abundantly, forms semi-circular clay ridge on kiva floor, joining kiva walls on each side of ventilator opening. The slab and adobe step thus formed rises 4 in. above kiva floor and is 1 ft. 2 in. wide.

Postholes: One found in northeast quadrant of kiva, a second in southeast quadrant. Both set ca. 3 ft. 6 in. in from kiva wall. (Presumably two others are in unexcavated section of kiva and a four-post roof support was employed.) Posthole in N.E. quadrant 6 in. diameter, 1 ft. 7 in. deep. Posthole in S.E. quadrant 9 in. diameter to depth of 10 in., 6 in. diameter to depth of 1 ft. 6 in.; suggests either wedged or double post.

Floor feature: Flat rock (8 in. by 5 in. by 1 in.) set into floor on south side of hearth; long axis parallel to hearth-ventilator axis. Center of stone 9 in. from clay rim of hearth.

Fill: Stained earth, ash, trash, fragmentary artifacts. Kiva was used as trash pit after abandonment; base of trash deposit fairly level, at depths of 3 ft. 10 in. to 4 ft. 10 in. below irregular ground surface. Analysis indicates marked homogeniety throughout, and trash deposit designated herein as "Level I". Underlain by ca. 1 ft. windblown sand (max. depth 4 ft. 10 in. to 5 ft. 8 in.); designated "Level II". "Level III" (max. depth 5 ft. 8 in. to 7 ft. 2 in.) consists of sand containing many charcoal flecks. Basal deposits ("Level IV", max. depth 7 ft. 2 in. to 7 ft. 7 in.) also contains small stones and adobe fragments resting on floor, presumably indicative of roof-fall. Two burials located; one in fill and one in pit just outside east wall of kiva south of ventilator passage. (Described in later section.)

Pits

Four pits were found west of the room-block. Their location is shown in Fig. 2.

Pit A: Circular, bell-shaped. Minimum diameter (at top) 1 ft. 5 in., encountered 1 ft. 6 in. below surface. Maximum diameter (at bottom) 1 ft. 10 in. at 3 ft. 8 in. below surface. Contents: brown stained fill, bits of charcoal, no artifacts.

Pit B: Circular, straight sides. Dug later than Pit A and cuts through one edge of it. Diameter 4 ft. 11 in., depth 2 ft. 11 in.; encountered 3 in. below surface. Contents: brown fill, no artifacts.

Pit C: Circular, bell-shaped. Maximum diameter 1 ft. 10 in., depth 2 ft. 10 in. below surface. Slight change in character of fill at depth of 10 in. below surface may indicate original top of cist. Contents: brown fill, no artifacts.

Pit D: Large circular pit, straight sides. Diameter 6 ft., depth 4 ft. 6 in. below surface; encountered 1 ft. 3 in. below surface. Pit had been clay-lined, at least in part, and clay indicates burning. Contents: brown fill, bits of charcoal, burned clay, several fist-sized rocks, apparently burned.

Trenches

A number of exploratory trenches are not associated with any particular feature. Some trenches disclosed little if any material culture and no architectural remnants; other trenches disclosed a number of features. Trench designations have been maintained as descriptive devices in some cases, but in the field they were abandoned whenever an identifiable feature was disclosed. Trench 1 encompassed the northern half of the room-block; when the individual rooms became apparent, it was not possible to reassign all material from "Trench 1" to the individual rooms. Those trenches in which the various architectural features were disclosed are all shallow excavations, none being more than 1 ft. deep.

Since these trench numbers have been retained to designate find-spots in some cases, a brief description of them is given below:

Trench 1 encompasses room-block north of rooms 7 and 8

Trench 2 encompasses room-block south of rooms 5 and 6

Trench 3 east of room 9, site debris only

Trench 4 encompasses pits A, B, C, D

Trench 5 above western edge of kiva, shallow

Trench 6 above center of kiva, shallow

Trench 7 east of room 7, southeast of kiva, site debris

Trench 8 east of rooms, south of Tr. 7, sterile

Trench 9 northeast of Tr. 8, sterile

POTTERY
(See Figs. 3, Pl. 4 and 8)

Most of the sherds recovered came from the kiva fill. The major types of painted pottery (described below) are Red Mesa B/W and Kwahe'e B/W; the major surface modification on culinary sherds are neck-banded and corrugated. Kwahe'e B/W and corrugated culinary sherds, predominant in their classes, are generally interpreted in the Rio Grande area as immediately subsequent to Red Mesa B/W and neck-banded culinary sherds, respectively. At the Tesuque By-Pass Site, analysis suggests that Red Mesa B/W and vessels with neck-banding decreased in popularity but continued to be used during the period of Kwahe'e predominance. The paucity of ceramic remains in the lower levels of the kiva is such that this inference is by no means certain. In brief, stratigraphy offers no definite evidence of major changes in ceramic material through time.

Although I have received a great deal of help and excellent advice from Mr. Stanley Stubbs of the Laboratory of Anthropology, I am not yet satisfied with my ability to distinguish the various types of tempering material used in this pottery. In the following sections, small black inclusions and larger, platy, black inclusions possessing a hardness comparable to the paste are interpreted as "sherd temper"; harder black inclusions and hard white angular flecks (sandstone) are included in the category "crushed rock." Softer gray and yellow globular inclusions (evidently clay) are considered as part of the original paste, not as temper. Fresh breaks showing less than six minute particles of mica and/or one or two grains of rock (round or angular) per sq. cm. are interpreted as clay with little or no tempering added.

							ROOMS										KIVA						
	SURFACE	TRENCH 3	TRENCH 7	TRENCH 4	TRENCH 1	TRENCH 2	ROOM 1	RM 5 RECT. PART	RM 5 "D" PART	ROOM 6	ROOM 7	ROOM 8	ROOM 9	ROOM 10	ROOM 11	SUM, ROOMS	level 1	level 2	level 3	lev. 4 (floor)	other	sum, kiva	AREA A TOTAL
KWAHE'E B/W	9	0	0	1	0	3	0	0	0	0	3	3	1	1	0	8	152	19	2	1	16	190	211
KWAHE'E B/W ?	1	0	0	0	0	2	0	0	0	0	1	1	0	0	0	2	3				2	5	10
RED MESA B/W	4	0	0	0	0	1	0	0	0	0	0	0	0	0	0	0	10			1		11	16
RED MESA B/W ?	0	1	0	2	1	0	0	0	0	0	0	0	0	0	0	0	13	3			1	17	21
GALLUP B/W	0	0	0	0	0	0	0	0	0	1	0	0	0	0	0	1	3			1	1	5	6
FINE PASTE GRAY	6	0	0	0	0	1	0	1	0	0	0	0	0	0	0	1	40	3			2	45	53
COARSE PASTE GRAY	5	4	0	0	1	5	0	1	0	0	0	0	0	0	0	1	13	2			1	16	32
TRADE AND INTRUSIVE	1	0	0	0	0	0	0	0	0	0	0	1	0	0	0	1	4					4	6
UNIDENTIFIED B/W	1	7	0	1	0	2	0	0	0	0	0	0	0	0	0	0	11	2	1	1	1	16	27
OTHER (B/W ?)	3	0	0	0	0	0	0	0	0	0	0	0	0	0	0	0	6					6	9
POLISHED BROWN	1	0	0	0	0	0	0	0	0	0	0	0	3	0	0	3	4				1	5	9
sum	31	12	0	4	2	14	0	2	0	1	4	5	4	1	0	17	259	29	3	4	25	320	400
CORRUGATED	46	11	1	4	14	96	0	3	5	3	38	27	4	0	1	81	412	46	8	18	38	522	775
NECK-BANDED	17	1	4	5	13	4	3	0	2	2	0	0	3	0	0	10	68	9	2	6	10	95	149
NECK-RIBBED	0	0	0	0	0	0	0	0	0	0	0	0	0	0	0	0	1			10		11	11
INCISED	1	0	0	0	0	0	0	0	0	0	0	0	0	0	0	0	8					8	9
PUNCTATE	0	0	0	0	0	0	0	0	0	0	0	0	0	0	0	0	4					4	4
SCORED	1	0	0	0	0	0	0	0	0	0	0	0	0	0	0	0	1			1		2	3
HANDLES, MISC.	0	0	1	1	0	2	0	0	0	0	1	2	0	0	0	3	9	3		1		13	20
sum	65	12	6	10	27	102	3	3	7	5	39	29	7	0	1	94	503	58	10	36	48	655	971
PLAIN SURFACE	91	14	5	4	23	50	1	3	5	7	24	42	8	1	0	91	447	39	6	29	30	552	829
SUM (total)	187	38	11	18	52	166	4	8	12	13	67	76	19	2	1	202	1209	126	19	69	103	1527	2200

Figure 3 – Provenience of potsherds, Area A.

The predominant painted pottery is Kwahe'e B/W (Pl. I *a-h;* Pl. IV *a-d*). Red Mesa B/W (Pl. I *i-k*), Gallup-Chaco B/W (Pl. I *l-o*), Santa Fe B/W (1 sherd; Pl. I *p*), Mancos ? B/W (Pl. I *q*), Wingate B/R (1 sherd; Pl. I *r*), and unidentified B/W's (Pl. I *s-t*) also occur. Culinary wares (Pl. II) are plain-surfaced, neck-banded and corrugated. A few incised and punctate sherds were found. A major part of this discussion is devoted to the Kwahe'e B/W because it differs slightly from Mera's general description of this pottery (1935:5 ff) and I know of no detailed description of the type in print. The discussion applies only to Kwahe'e B/W from this site and, insofar as it concerns jars and ollas, is based on but a few partially reconstructed vessels.

Painted Sherds

Kwahe'e B/W (Pl. I *a-h;* Pl. IV *a-d*): For comments on spatial and temporal distribution, see Fig. 13, also Mera, 1935; Stubbs and Stallings, 1953. Constructed by coiling and scraping. Thickness from .18 to .30 in. (4.6-7.6 *mm.*), average *ca.* .22 in. (5.6 *mm.*) The paste is quite uniform; it is homogeneous, gray, hard to medium-hard, with occasional yellow (clay?) inclusions, unground gray clay, bits of mica, sand and/or angular rock. (In this respect the collection apparently differs from the Kwahe'e B/W described by Mera as usually sherd tempered.) Sherds break with a fracture that varies in appearance from very smooth to somewhat sandy under a ten power glass. The majority (78 per cent) of the sherds have no temper or only occasional grains of sand or rock visible to the naked eye or under a ten power glass; some specimens (17 per cent) have finely ground sherd temper and others (5 per cent) have ground rock temper. These latter materials, when used, were added sparingly. Scraping marks are usually smoothed, especially on bowls and jar exteriors. A thin, streaky white slip is applied to bowl interiors and jar exteriors, but not to bowl exteriors or jar interiors. (One bowl sherd of typical paste but atypical design has the thin slip carried over the lip and down the outside for *ca.* 0.5 in. [13 mm]). The pottery is decorated with mineral paint which ranges in color from black to rust-red but is, typically, a dark reddish black. Designs are of a crudely executed, heavy-lined Chaco tradition. The most common decorative element is a band of diagonal hatchure with lines .05 to .13 in. (1.3-3.3 mm.) wide, averaging *ca.* .08 to .10 in. (2.0-2.5 mm.), with framing lines of the same width as the hatchure lines or slightly thicker. Series of parallel lines, solid triangles, diagonal bands of parallel lines with exterior pendant right triangles, horizontal bands with opposed and offset equilateral triangles, checkerboards (with and without dots), wide-line multiple chevrons, and triangles with pendant ticking also occur. Curvilinear designs are very rare. There is only one example of a painted lip.

Bowl interiors are decorated within a horizontal zone which begins at or near the lip (Fig. 4B, *a-c*). The width of this band varies considerably, but the bottom of bowls is never painted. Two bowl sherds show two short parallel diagonal lines on the exterior just below the lip. Ollas are decorated in a band which begins just below the inflection point of the neck and ends at a point slightly below the maximum diameter of the vessel (Fig. 4B, *e*). Jars (only 1 definite example) are decorated within a wide band from the lip to a point just below the maximum diameter (Fig. 4B, *d*). Lineal borders and framing lines usually occur, but are often incorporated into the design.

Although no complete vessels were found, bowls, ollas, and possibly jars, are represented. The single jar fragment is sherd tempered and fits Mera's description of Kwahe'e. Sherd tempered Kwahe'e is not common at this site however, and the vessel may not be of local manufacture. Of the painted sherds classified as Kwahe'e B/W, 121 (62 per cent) were painted on the concave surface and are presumably from bowls, 74 (38 per cent) are painted on the convex surface and are presumably from ollas or jars. A maximum of 95 bowls and 45 ollas and/or jars is represented; the actual number is probably smaller in both cases.

Red Mesa B/W (Pl. I *i-k*); *Gallup B/W* (Pl. I *l-m*): Sherds classified as Red Mesa and Gallup B/W differ in many respects from the Kwahe'e B/W. The paste of the former types is less homogeneous and fresh fractures appear not smooth, but jagged or chunky when viewed in cross section under a ten power glass. Many sherds have a dark central core, others have a uniformly gray cross section. Crushed rock (including most of the "white flecks") and sherd temper are added in medium amounts; usually both types of temper occur in a single sherd. Mica inclusions appear in but one example. Designs are more finely drawn, bowl exteriors are almost invariably covered with a fair to medium white slip; lips, with two exceptions, are painted black.

The distinction between Red Mesa B/W and Gallup B/W rests on design style: following Wendorf (*in* Wendorf, Fox, and Lewis, 1956: 5-6), sherds with a rather thick-lined Kana-a style decoration are called Red Mesa B/W, sherds with Dogoszhi style decoration are classed as Gallup B/W.

Although sherds of Red Mesa B/W and Gallup-Chaco B/W are found in many early sites in the northern Rio Grande Valley, they presumably represent trade pieces rather than objects of local manufacture.

Other Painted Pottery: Identified intrusives have been listed above. The unidentified B/W sherds are decorated with mineral paint (four exceptions from a single vessel, which may represent a transitional Kwahe'e-Santa Fe B/W). As a class they are tempered more heavily than Kwahe'e B/W, usually with crushed sherd, and mica inclusions are rare. These sherds show considerable variation in design, but all differ from those styles characteristic of Red Mesa, Gallup, and Kwahe'e B/W.

Unpainted Sherds

Unpainted Gray Sherds; non-culinary: Sherds described as "fine paste, gray" are unpainted fragments possessing a paste similar to that of Kwahe'e B/W. Such sherds are probably unpainted portions of Kwahe'e vessels. No rim sherds of this class were found. "Coarser paste, gray" refers to all other unpainted fragments of non-culinary gray pottery. These could be from unpainted portions of Red Mesa, Gallup-Chaco, and/or unidentified B/W vessels. No rim sherds of this class were found.

Other Unpainted Sherds; culinary: The great majority of the culinary sherds (neck-banded, corrugated, and plain-surfaced) seem to have been made from a common paste tempered with crushed rock. This paste, presumably local, is described below:

Local culinary paste: —soft to medium hard; rather porous; fresh break viewed in cross section is rough, produces a crumbly fracture and, under a ten power glass, frequently shows transverse laminations of the coil. Color is usually black or dark brown; some tans and grays occur. Brown paste with a black core also appears. Temper, used in medium to liberal amounts, consists of coarsely crushed rock, primarily quartz and quartzite. Mica inclusions are very common. Surfaces are well-smoothed, but temper frequently protrudes and flakes of mica are usually visible on both surfaces. Surface color ranges from black through tan to gray, with blacks and tans most common. Black exteriors are normal (due to use in many cases), interiors are usually black or tan. Sherds range in thickness from .08 to .15 in. (2.0-3.8 mm.), averaging .10 to .12 in. (2.5-3.0 mm.).

The breaking strength, breaking pattern, types of inclusions, temper, and general appearance of this paste are fairly uniform and I do not feel that type divisions on the basis of paste or temper would be legitimate. All sherds discussed below are of this paste unless noted otherwise.

Neck-banded (P. II a-c): –All apparently rim, neck, and side sherds; no bases. Of the 149 sherds, 24 are rim sherds. There are several methods of treating bands. Most commonly, bands are .4 to .5 in. (10.5-12.5 mm.) wide (from one coil juncture to next, not actual coil width) and are unmodified (Pl. II *a*); (65 sherds including 10 rims). One specimen in this class has sherd temper. Often the actual coil juncture was obliterated (Pl. II *b*) (46 sherds including 7 rims). Quite a few (35 sherds including 6 rims) have beveled bands (Pl. II c). The short bevel was produced on the lower portion of the coil by drawing a flat object around the coil; the plane of the bevel slopes down and inward.

Three sherds, including one rim, have either narrow coils or an unusually great overlap. The neck-bands measure .17 to .20 in. (4.3-5.1 mm.) between coil lines. These sherds may be no more than small fragments from corrugated vessels with extremely shallow indentations.

Eight sherds (no rims or bottoms) can be described as "banded-incised." These specimens have either a flat exterior surface or very little lateral overlap. Coil (?) lines have been emphasized by incision. Five sherds have incisions ranging from .32 to .50 in. (8.1-12.7 mm.) apart. Three have incisions from .20 to .25 (5.1-6.4 mm.) apart. Perhaps these latter could have been called "ribbed-incised" more appropriately.

Of the whole collection of neck-banded sherds, only one indicates that coil overlap was on the inside going up the vessel. All other sherds showing termination of banding indicate that coil overlap was on the outside.

Corrugated (Pl. II d-e; *Pl. VIII* a): –Apparently made of the same paste as the neck-banded sherds, the corrugated sherds differ in several respects. The distance between coil lines averages less in the corrugated sherds, sherds from the lower portions and bottoms of vessels are present, and the amount of temper appears to be slightly less than that of the neck-banded sherds.

There is considerable variation in the execution of the corrugation. The "typical" corrugated sherd (e.g. Pl. II *e*) from the collection has shallow (.03 in., or 0.7 mm., or less) finger indentation of coils that are ca. .25 in. (6.4 mm.) wide. Lateral overlap, defined as the distance from the actual coil juncture to the greatest protrusion of the upper coil, is slight, ca. .02 in. (0.5 mm.). By the very nature of the indentations, their vertical placement is not entirely random; arrangement to produce a pattern, however, is rare. These patterns occur almost invariably as lineal segments which are either vertical or which incline upward to the right. Coils are overlapped on the outside. Smoothing of the coil lines or the corrugations may or may not be present.

Variation in all characteristics of the "typical corrugated sherd" is to be found; in depth of indentation, width of coil, lateral overlap, degree of regularity in placement of indentations, and amount of post-indentation smoothing. This variation is, for the most part, continuous, and only one sub-group (21 sherds) is distinctive (Pl. II *d*). This consists of sherds with deep (.17-.14 in., or 3.6-4.3 mm.) regularly spaced indentations, giving an impression of either vertical lines, diagonals slanting up to the right, or (1 sherd only) diagonals slanting up to the left. There are no basal sherds in this sub-group; one rim sherd is present.

Five corrugated sherds have their coil lines accentuated by incision. These sherds are all of medium band width, have very shallow indentations, and very little lateral overlap.

Three sherds have corrugations produced with a blunt stick or by some means other than the finger. (It would be difficult to say with assurance how many other sherds were corrugated in a similar fashion.)

One sherd with typical corrugation has been scored with a blunt stick. The scoring marks are perpendicular to the coil lines.

Miscellaneous culinary; surface altered:

Neck-ribs: —Eleven sherds from two vessels (Pl. II g). These ribs differ from neck-bands in having been formed by round coils rather than flat ones. Coil lines have been accentuated by incision, and the ribs themselves appear almost semicircular in cross section. The ribs in one vessel range in width from .25 to .36 in. (6.4-9.1 mm.), averaging ca. .30 in. (7.6 mm.); in the other they range from .15 to .25 in. (3.8-6.4 mm.), averaging *ca.* .24 in. (6.1 mm.). The ribs protrude .07 to .11 in. (1.8-2.8 mm.) from the coil line.

Incised: —Nine sherds from four vessels (jars?) have incised exteriors. Seven (from two vessels) are incised in a herring-bone, or nested chevron, design (Pl. IV *e-f*). In one case it can be ascertained that the incision covered only the upper portion of a jar. These incisions are fairly deep and seem to have been made with either a stick or a thumb-nail. One sherd from another vessel shows light linear incision (Pl. II *h*). The sherd from the fourth vessel shows incisions in the form of concentric diamonds (Pl. II *i*). The incisions forming the edges of the diamonds do not meet at the vertices. All of these sherds seem to be of local paste, but the chevron-incised sherds have an unusual amount of mica in them, visible both in fresh breaks and on the surface.

Punctate: —Four sherds, probably from one vessel (jar?) (Pl. II f). The punctations are ovate but pointed at both ends, and are quite uniform; *ca.* .45 in. (11.4 mm.) long, .20 in. (5.1 mm.) maximum width, *ca.* .08 in. (2.0 mm.) deep. They slant up to the right at an angle of about 45 degrees and are placed one above another; the effect produced is that of diagonal lines slanting upward to the right. The impressions may have been made with a stick; more probably, they were made with a thumb-nail. This decoration was confined to the upper portion of the vessel. Apparently of local paste, although two sherds have a gray core with a dark central streak. (Gray cores occur in what is presumed to be local ware, but are not typical.)

Scored: —Three sherds, apparently from different vessels, have scored exteriors. No rims; one sherd may be from the bottom of a vessel.

Plain surface: —829 sherds of plain-surfaced culinary ware, made from local paste, were recovered. Fifty-nine were rim sherds, 23 were from bases. Other sherds were originally parts of large vessels with gently recurved sides. One sherd indicated a cylindrical neck on a globular vessel, and two sherds were from vessels with a sharp shoulder. No complete vessels were recovered, but an examination of the sherds allows certain generalizations.

All sherds are smooth, although ten specimens have very rough, lumpy surfaces and were smoothed just enough to remove the coil lines. Surface color is as described under "local culinary paste." Seven sherds, apparently from unused vessels, have a yellow-tan color similar to that of the present-day culinary ware made in Taos, Picuris, and Nambe. It may be that many, if not most, of the culinary vessels from this site were of this color originally.

These sherds represent not only plain-surfaced vessels, but also the lower portions of neck-banded, ribbed, corrugated, punctate, and incised vessels. I am unable to assign sherds to any particular category in most cases. Vessels in the five last-named categories have rims that are smooth for .50 to *ca.* 1.25 in. (13 to *ca.* 32 mm.) below the orifice. Of the 59 rim sherds classed as "plain surface" only five large specimens are definitely from smooth surface vessels. Twenty other rim sherds show a smooth surface finished for 1.0 to 1.5 in. (25-38 mm.) below the orifice and are probably from plain-surfaced vessels. Two rim sherds are from specialized vessels; a seed-jar and a hand-modeled globular jar with a cylindrical neck. It is impossible to say whether the remaining 32 "plain rim sherds" are from plain-surfaced vessels, neck-banded vessels, etc.

The following remarks apply equally to any of the six categories of culinary ware mentioned above: Sherds which were from bases of vessels indicate that rounded bases and flat bases predominated. It is possible that slightly pointed bases occurred, but none of the basal sherds recovered were of sufficient size to enforce this supposition. One sherd indicated a flat base with a concave circular indentation into the exterior, at the very bottom of the vessel. Basal sherds range in thickness from .5 to .6 in. (13-15 mm.) and side sherds are about half this thick. All culinary vessels seem to have had slightly flaring rims. As noted above, gently recurved sides were typical; sharp shoulders and definite breaks between body and neck were not.

Miscellaneous culinary; plain surface: —Nine sherds of nonlocal brownware paste were recovered.

Three sherds from one vessel were well-smoothed but not polished. The temper was crushed white rock (probably quartzite); grains were small to medium in size and were added liberally. The paste is fairly homogeneous and brown in cross section with a slightly darker central streak; surface color is orange-brown. Thickness .25 in. (6.4 mm.). There are no inclusions of mica.

Six sherds were polished on the exterior. They were made of a fairly fine paste, soft to medium hard. A medium amount of crushed rock temper was used. Five sherds (all of which may be from different vessels) were .20 in. (5.1 mm.) thick. One of these was a rim sherd. The sixth sherd was .25 to .30 in. (6.4-7.6 mm.) thick and apparently came from the side of a vessel. Four of these polished brownware sherds show what appear to be very small flecks of mica on their surfaces.

Handles: —Twenty whole or fragmentary handles were recovered; ten strap handles, seven lugs, and three rope handles. The strap handles are, with one exception, fairly large (Pl. II *j*). Outside maximum dimensions vary from 2.5 to 3.5 in. (64-89 mm.), width is *ca.* 1.0 in. (25 mm.). The small strap handle has a maximum dimension of

1.6 in. (40.5 mm.) and is 0.7 in. (17.8 mm.) wide. One of the large strap handles had been attached vertically, with one end just below the lip of the vessel. Two others seem to have been attached horizontally near vessel shoulders. Orientation and place of attachment of the others could not be ascertained.

Of the seven lugs, five are conical, with a slight downward curve at the tip (Pl. II *m*). These were attached to vessels near the rim. A sixth lug was large and elliptical in side view, with the long axis of the ellipse horizontal. This horizontal axis measured 1.25 in. (31.7 mm.), the vertical axis 0.7 in. (17.8 mm.), thickness 0.5 in. (12.7 mm.). It was attached to the vessel by a short 0.4 in. (10.4 mm.) stem, apparently near the lip. The exterior surface of this lug is concave (Pl. II *l*). The seventh lug was a curved strip of clay ca. 2.5 in. (64 mm.) long, 1.2 in. (30 mm.) maximum vertical width, 0.7 in. (18 mm.) thick, which was attached to the vessel horizontally (Pl. II *k*). The strip had been modelled so that its upper surface was convex, its lower surface concave, the result was a handle similar to those often found on contemporary desk drawers.

The rope handles were fragmentary. Two were single coil with maximum diameters of .68 and .69 in. (17.2 and 17.6 mm.). The third was composed of two parallel coils, each *ca.* .38 in. (9.7 mm.) in diameter (Pl. II *n*).

Artifacts; ceramic

Scrapers: –Seven sherds were recovered which had one or more edges smoothed from use.

Five sherds show that use was probably in a direction perpendicular to the face of the sherd. Kwahe'e B/W (Pl. II *r*), corrugated, fine paste gray, and plain sherds are represented. One example is shaped in the form of an isosceles triangle, is smoothed along all edges, and has a hole drilled in the vertex opposite the base (Pl. II s). Two other sherds are square; one shows use along one edge, the other, along two adjacent edges. The remaining two sherds are irregularly shaped and show use on one edge only.

One large Kwahe'e B/W olla sherd, roughly square, shows use along one edge and also on the opposite edge and adjoining exterior surface.

The seventh specimen is semicircular. It is smooth along the entire arc of the circle and was evidently broken along a diameter.

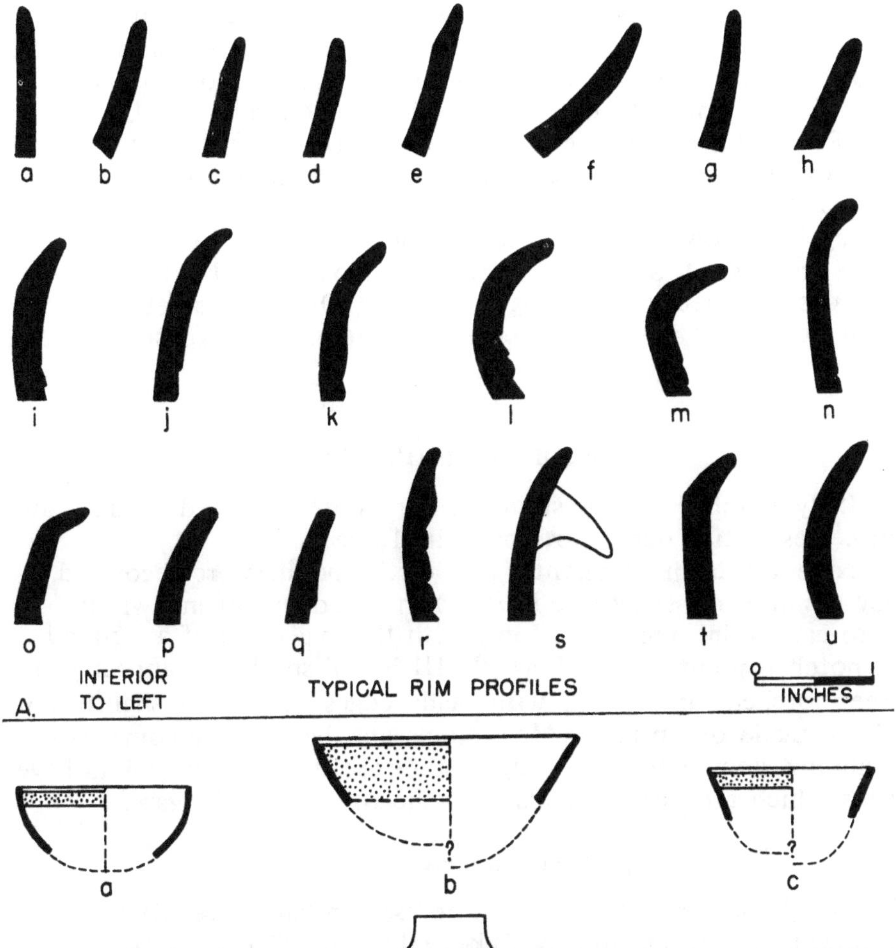

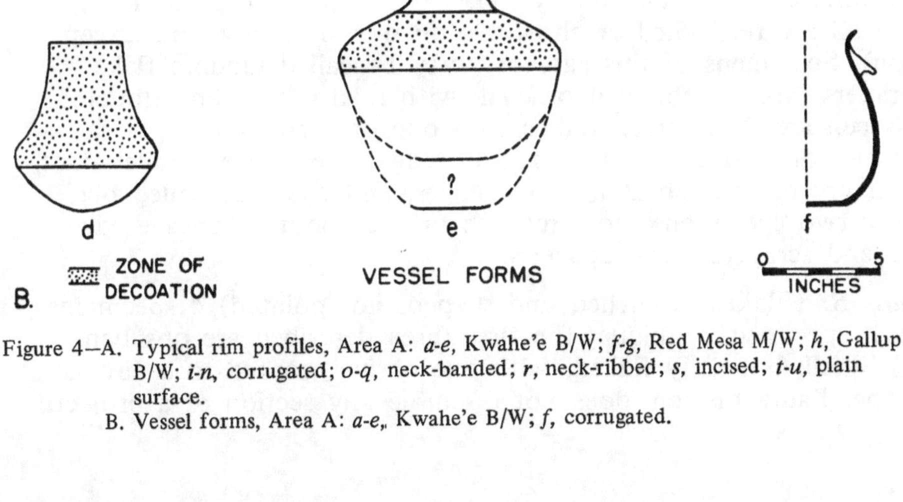

Figure 4—A. Typical rim profiles, Area A: *a-e*, Kwahe'e B/W; *f-g*, Red Mesa M/W; *h*, Gallup B/W; *i-n*, corrugated; *o-q*, neck-banded; *r*, neck-ribbed; *s*, incised; *t-u*, plain surface.

B. Vessel forms, Area A: *a-e*,, Kwahe'e B/W; *f*, corrugated.

Pipes: 1) Room 5. Curved cloud-blower (Pl. II *o*), fine culinary paste, exterior well-smoothed, undecorated. Length along central axis 3.58 in. Outside diameter: bit .35 in., bowl .80 in. Interior bowl diameter .55 in., depth of bowl 1.31 in. Dottle found in bowl.

2) Room 9, floor. Straight cloud-blower (Pl. II *q*), fine culinary paste, exterior well-smoothed, undecorated. Length 2.75 in. Outside diameter: bit .32 in. bowl .80 in. Interior bowl diameter .65 in., depth of bowl .80 in. Dottle found in bowl.

3) Kiva, Level I. Straight stubby cloud-blower (Pl. II *p*), fine culinary paste, undecorated. Length 1.60 in., Outside diameter: bit .35 in., bowl .70 in. Interior bowl diameter .65 in. No signs of use.

ARTIFACTS OF STONE

Projectile Points (Pl. III *a-i*)

Only notched and/or stemmed forms are discussed in this category. Descriptive details are given in Table 2.

Nine whole or fragmentary projectile points were recovered. They are all small (length .57-*ca.* .90 in., median .80 in., width .40 to ca. .74 in., median .50 in.) With the exception of a serrated side-notched point of red chert (Pl. III *b*), all specimens appear to be corner-notched, unserrated, with blade edges straight or slightly convex, and are made of obsidian. Most stems and bases are missing; two expanding stems and one straight stem are intact. Two points have blades which are nearly equilateral; the others are elongate.

Other Chipped Stone

Class A: (Flakes showing retouch or use; unshaped. Pl. III *j-k*) 41 specimens. All are apparently flakes (three possible exceptions), and all are retouched or show use on one side only (one exception). Specimens of this category may be called random flake scrapers. Six are rounded or oval, with relatively steep retouch. Sixteen are fairly thick flakes with one or more thin edges showing use or retouch on one or more edges. Five have parallel sides, with use or retouch along these edges, and could be called blades. Only two specimens show retouch or use about a concave edge. No end scrapers were recovered.

Class B: (Flakes retouched and shaped, not pointed) 4 specimens. Each specimen is unique; the first three described are obsidian.
(a) Small, bifacially flaked, with one corner worked to a circular shape. Badly broken; does not resemble any section of a projectile

TABLE 2

PROJECTILE POINT DIMENSIONS, AREA A
(In Inches)

Reference Plate III	NOTCHES		STEM			BLADE EDGE			LENGTH	WIDTH	THICKNESS	MATERIAL	LOCUS
	COR NER	SIDE	EX PAN.	STR.	CONTR.	CONV.	STR.	CONC.					
b	. . .	x	?	?	?	s x s	. . .	. . .	(.90)	.64	.16	Red chert	Rm. No. 7 floor
a	?	?	?	?	?	x	. . .	. . .	(.90)	.50	.10	Obsd.	Rm. No. 5
e	x	. . .	x	. . .	. . .	. . .	x	. . .	(.85)	(.42)	.13	Obsd.	Surf.
i	?	?	?	?	?	. . .	x	. . .	(.85)	(.74)	.11	Obsd.	Surf.
g	x	. . .	x	. . .	. . .	x	x	. . .	.80	(.43)	.09	Obsd.	Surf.
f	?	?	?	?	?	x	. . .	. . .	(.75)	.40	.10	Obsd.	Surf.
d	x	. . .	x?	x?	. . .	x	. . .	. . .	(.73)	.46	.10	Obsd.	Kiva, Floor
c	x	. . .	x	. . .	. . .	. . .	. . .	x	.60	(.56)	.10	Obsd.	Tr. 2
h	x	. . .	x	. . .	. . .	x	. . .	. . .	.57	(.52)	.14	Obsd.	Surf.

Note: — x = present
s x s = present, both edges serrate
(-) = estimated dimension

TABLE 3
LOCUS OF CHIPPED STONE ARTIFACTS, AREA A

LOCUS/CLASS	A	B	B'	C	D	E	F	TOTALS
Surface	12	1	3	0	15	0	0	31
Trench 3	1	0	0	1	0	2	0	4
Trench 7	0	0	0	0	0	0	0	0
Trench 4	1	0	0	0	0	0	0	1
Trench 1	2	0	0	0	2	1	0	5
Trench 2	3	0	0	0	2	0	0	5
Room 1	1	0	0	0	0	0	0	1
Room 5, rect. part	3	0	0	0	3	0	0	6
Room 5, "D" part	1	0	0	1	2	0	1	5
Room 6	0	0	0	0	0	0	0	0
Room 7	3	0	0	0	2	0	1	6
Room 8	4	0	0	0	1	1	0	6
Room 9	0	0	0	1	2	1	0	4
Room 10	1	0	0	0	3	1	2	7
Room 11	0	0	0	0	0	0	0	0
Kiva, level 1	4	3	3	1	14	0	0	25
Kiva, level 2	0	0	0	0	0	0	0	0
Kiva, level 3	2	0	0	0	1	0	0	3
Kiva, level 4	2	0	0	0	1	0	2	5
Kiva, other	1	0	1	1	0	0	0	3
Totals	41	4	7	5	48	6	6	117

point (Pl. III *l*). (b) Elongate, bifacially flaked, coming to a rounded point. Relatively thick in cross section. Probably a drill (Pl. III *m*). (c) Irregular flake, worked on one side to a rounded point. Indications of use along one edge and around point (Pl. III *o*). Possibly an end scraper for fine work. (d) Rectangular object of quartzite, shallowly flaked on both sides. All edges fairly sharp. Probably a scraper (Pl. III *n*).

Class B': (Flakes shaped and retouched to a point. Pl III *p-u*) seven specimens. One fairly thick flake worked on one face only; two flakes (both obsidian) retouched on one face only; four thin flakes worked on both sides; all obsidian. Triangular and quadrangular in shape. No indications of hafting.

Class C: (Unretouched flake, jagged edge) five specimens. All are fairly large; two may be small cores. No indications of use, but would be suitable for cutting.

Class D: (Random flakes; edges smooth, not sharply pointed, no retouch) 48 specimens.

Class E: (Sharply pointed random flakes, no retouch) 6 specimens. These flakes are of sizes comparable to the specimens in category B', and would have been included therein if they had shown any signs of use.

Class F: (Cores, or possibly thick, heavily chipped flakes) six specimens. Five smaller specimens, none with any dimension greater than 1.5 in. One larger specimen is a crude right circular cone with flake scars along the sides. Height 1.6 in., diameter of base 1.9 to 2.3 in.

Metates and Manos

No complete metates were found, but some fragments permit estimates of original dimensions. All manos and metates are of granite unless noted otherwise.

Trough metates, open at one end: 1) Kiva, Levels I and II. Fragments of metate originally 2 ft. 6 in. long, 1 ft. 4 in. wide, (maximum) height 5.5 in. Trough rectangular with rounded ends, 1 ft. 9 in. long, 8.3 in. wide; maximum depth below distal end. 4.0 in.

2) Kiva, Level I. Fragment of metate originally about 1 ft. wide. Other dimensions not determinable. Trough rectangular with rounded ends, *ca.* .10 in. wide and 4 in. deep.

3) Kiva, Level I. Fragment of metate originally closed at one end, 5 in. thick. No other measurements ascertainable. Trough probably rectangular with rounded ends; may have been elliptical.

4) Kiva, Level I. Fragment of metate originally closed at one end, 5 in. thick. No other exterior dimensions determinable. Trough elliptical, *ca.* 10 in. wide.

Trough metates, open at one or both ends: 5) Kiva, Level III. Proximal fragment of metate, open at end. Its distal portion, also with an open end, was found on floor of kiva. Metate 1 ft. 9 in. long, 11.5 in. wide, 7 in. thick. Grinding area, whose surface area had decreased with use, has straight sides converging toward proximal end. Maximum length of grinding surface 1 ft. 7 in., maximum width 8 in., maximum depth 5 in.

6) Kiva, Level IV. Fragment; width at least 1 ft. 5 in., height 6 in. Trough apparently rectangular with rounded ends, slightly undercut, at least 1 ft. wide; 5 in. deep. Lava.

Basin metates: 7) Fragment of oval metate, *ca.* 2 ft. 3 in. long, 1 ft. 3 in. wide, 6.5 in. maximum thickness. Elliptical grinding depression, estimated dimensions 1 ft. 3 in. long, 9 in. wide, 3 in. deep.

8) West of Room 1, at depth 7 in. Fragment of oval metate 6 in. thick. Depression 2 in. maximum depth.

Manos: 1-4) Kiva. Level I. Four manos, rectangular with rounded corners. Length 8 to 10 in., width 5 to 6 in., thickness 1.0 to 1.5 in. Two rectangular in cross section; the third has air-foil cross section; the fourth, with one long edge rounded, has thick air-foil cross section. The thinner air-foil shaped mano appears to have been used on two surfaces, the others on one surface only.

5) Room 7. Rectangular mano with rounded corners. Air-foil cross section; 7.5 in. long, 4 in. wide, 1 in. maximum thickness. Convex face shows wear, flat face does not.

Axes, Mauls and Hammerstones

Axe: room 6 (Pl. IV *h*). Two side notches .30 in. deep, one basal notch .21 in. deep. Made from flat stone, chipped roughly around edges to shape. Smoothing at one of the side notches and on both faces near the cutting edge. Length from cutting edge to line joining basal extremities 3.65 in.; maximum width (above notches) 3.30 in.; maximum thickness .65 in.; thickness .25 in. from cutting edge *ca.* .25 in.

Mauls: Kiva, Level I. All full-grooved at or near center of maul.

One made from section of lava metate (Pl. IV *i*). 4.9 in. long; butt end 3.5 in. high, 3.1 in. thick; front tapers to 2.0 in. in height, 1.7 in. thick. Shaped by pecking.

Second made of lava, fragmentary (Pl. IV. *g*). Apparently it was fairly symmetric; 5.0 in. long, 4.0 in. high, 2.0 in. maximum thickness. Shaped by pecking and breaking.

Third made from granite boulder, fragmentary (Pl. IV *j*). Apparently symmetrical, 3.8 in. long, 3.3 in. high, 2.6 in. thick. Some indication of pecking.

Hammerstone: (Room 7) Battered stone, roughly spherical, with diameters from 2.2 to 3.8 in.

ARTIFACTS OF BONE

Awls or Flakers

Twelve – all apparently made from mammal leg-bone.

Class A: Head of bone intact, four specimens. Three are ulnas; two from antelope (Kiva, levels I and IV; Pl. III *ff* and *ee*) and one from a deer (Kiva, level I; Pl. III *dd*). The fourth (Kiva, level IV; Pl. III *bb*) is a longbone from a young unidentified mammal, with the epiphesial cap missing.

Class B: Head unaltered except for original splitting, one specimen; (Kiva, level I; Pl. III *aa*). Evidently a split antelope metapodial.

Class C: Head partly worked down, 3 three specimens; room 5, (Pl. III *y*); Kiva, level I, (Pl. III *z*); Kiva indeterminate. Made from split long-bones, none identified. Heads are all fragmentary and apparently were worked down to some extent.

Class D: No awls were found which had the articular head worked completely away.

Class E: Splinter awls, two doubtful specimens; Kiva, level I and Kiva indeterminate (Pl. III *cc*). These are formed from split mammal leg bones and show no sign of being worked beyond the original splitting. If these are truly artifacts, they should be placed in category A above.

Class F: Unidentified, two specimens from room 7 (Pl. III *w-x*). Two distal fragments with articular heads missing. Both unidentified mammal long-bone.

Bird Bone Whistle: (Tr. 2; Pl. III *gg*)

Bone cut perpendicular to long axis and smoothed. 2.81 in. long. Hole cut near center of shaft, diameter .20 in.

Split Deer Metapodial: (Kiva, level I; Pl. III *ii*)

Split lengthwise, proximal portion broken off. Bone well smoothed across split, producing fairly sharp edges from a point 2.50 in. below distal end to break. Length 6.60 in.; width below condyle .61 in., thickness .45 in. Width at break .81 in., thickness .26 in. This specimen could have functioned as a weaving tool.

Cut Bone

From unidentified large bird: (Kiva, level I; Pl. III *hh*): cut perpendicular to long axis at one end, several deep grooves parallel to cut near end. No sign of working.

ARTIFACTS OF SHELL

One specimen, from Trench 2 (Pl. III *v*): a crudely shaped triangular piece of shell, with one vertex broken.

BURIALS

Two burials were found; one in the kiva fill and one in a pit just outside the southeast edge of the kiva.

Burial 1 was located at a depth of 3 ft. 6 in. below surface in the northeast portion of the kiva. The burial had been deposited in a pit dug in the trashy fill of the kiva. The pit was subsequently filled with the same material. The skeleton was flexed on its right side, with its head to the northeast. The head was twisted into an upright position, facing northwest. The burial was that of an infant. There is some indication of lambdoidal or occipital deformation. A small turquoise bead was found near the right ear, and a pierced or "killed" shell was found in front of the shoulder portion of the skeleton.

Burial 2 (excavated by Peckham) was located in a pit originally excavated to 5 ft. below surface just outside the southeast wall of the kiva. The burial pit was 4 ft. 6 in. along an axis roughly parallel to the kiva wall, and 3 ft. 2 in. wide. The skeleton was lying on its back, semiflexed, with its knees up. Its head was to the northeast, looking upward. The skeleton is probably that of an adult female. There is some lambdoidal deformation. No burial goods were recovered. (Portions of a third burial were recovered from the general site area during subsequent construction activities by the New Mexico State Highway Department. The skeleton was evidently that of a young adult male; no skull was recovered. (Cf. "3294-3" in Reed, 1957: 89, 97.)

AREA B

ARCHITECTURE

Dwelling Area

In Area B there was encountered a conglomeration of architectural remains which were difficult to interpret. Patches of clay floor, bits of walls, and pits were found. Their placement is shown in Figure 5. A kiva was located some 90 ft. southeast of the dwelling area; its eastern quadrant was excavated.

Indications of at least three, and probably four, levels of occupation were found. The most recent occupation was marked by slab-based walls and patches of floor. These floor areas were quite near the ground surface and were poorly preserved. I was unable to find a well-defined room-block. From one of these walls several adobe bricks were recovered. One complete (rectangular) brick, which had one flat face and one convex face, measured 5 in. by 4 in. by 3 in. maximum thickness.

A second series of wall-lines was found which passed, in part, beneath the slab-based walls. These walls were of adobe, and were neither parallel nor perpendicular to the slab-based walls. Patches of clay floor were also found in association with these walls.

Four relatively large circular features were found in the wall-and-floor area (Features A-D, Figure 5).

Feature A appears to be the remains of a roundish pit structure. It is located below an adobe wall and its associated floor, and also below a slab-based wall. Its floor is 7 ft. 6 in. to 8 ft. 6 in. in diameter and 2 ft. 11 in. below surface.

Two hearth areas were associated with Feature A. One, *ca.* 1 ft. 6 in. in diameter, was located near the wall in the southeast quadrant of the structure; a second with diameters 1 ft. 5 in.-2 ft. was located above the floor of Feature B, and outside the

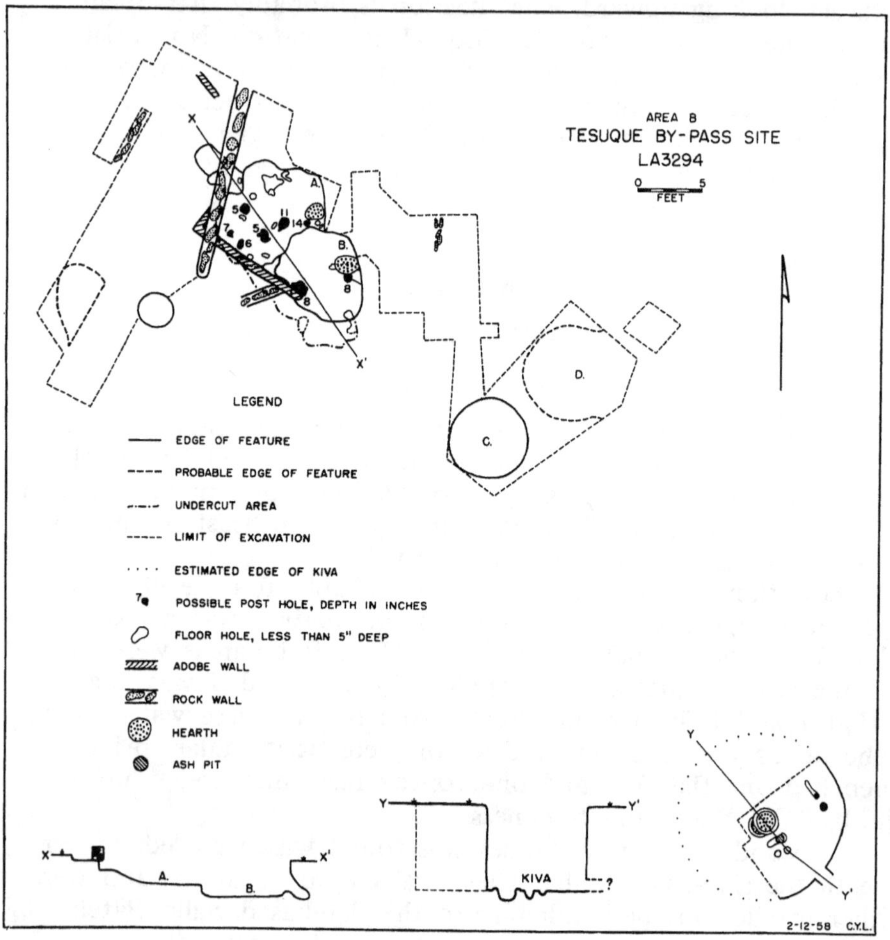
AREA B
TESUQUE BY-PASS SITE
LA3294
0 5
FEET
LEGEND
EDGE OF FEATURE
PROBABLE EDGE OF FEATURE
UNDERCUT AREA
LIMIT OF EXCAVATION
ESTIMATED EDGE OF KIVA
POSSIBLE POST HOLE, DEPTH IN INCHES
FLOOR HOLE, LESS THAN 5" DEEP
ADOBE WALL
ROCK WALL
HEARTH
ASH PIT
A.
B.
C.
D.
KIVA
2-12-58 C.Y.L.

Figure 5

south wall of Feature A, but at the floor level of Feature A. Both hearth areas were marked by concentrations of ash and burned rock; no prepared basin or rimmed hearth occurred.

Apparently there was an entrance on the north side of the feature. The pit floor sloped up to the entry floor, which terminated in a step. The entrance passage was 3 ft. 4 in. long, 2 ft. 4 in. wide, and the step was 10 in. high (see Figure 5).

No regular posthole pattern was discovered; there were no peripheral posts. Holes filled with bits of charcoal and wood were concentrated in the central portion of the feature, and there is a suggestion of two short parallel rows of posts, 2 to 3 ft. apart, running east and west.

Feature B is adjacent to Feature A. Also roundish, its floor is 6.0 to 8.0 ft. in diameter and 1 ft. below the floor of Feature A. The only floor features were two holes, *ca.* 10 in. in diameter, 8 in. deep, located on opposite ends of a diameter of the feature and set in from the walls *ca.* 1 ft. 6 in. (see Figure 5). No hearth or entry was found. Some flakes were found in the fill just above the floor of Feature B; no sherds were definitely associated with this structure.

Feature C was a clay-lined saucer-shaped depression. It had a well-defined clay floor which sloped upward at its perimeter. Its diameter was 7 ft. 6 in., and depth below surface 1 ft. 7 in. No postholes, ash areas, or floor features were found.

Feature D was roughly circular and located a few feet northeast of Feature C (Figure 5). Its clay floor, not well-defined, was *ca.* 9 ft. in diameter. Sterile soil was reached 2 ft. 5 in. below ground surface. A fragmentary patch of floor, about 1 foot square, was found 1 ft. 10 in. below ground surface. A flat piece of rock, similar in form to a ventilator slab, was found lying horizontally in the black stained fill at a depth of 1 ft. Several fire-stained, fist-sized rocks were also found at this depth. There were no postholes or ash areas.

Kiva

Approximately one-fourth of the kiva in Area B was excavated (Pl. II *b*). It was apparently circular, diameter *ca.* 16 ft.

Walls: Clay, *ca.* 8 in. thick, covered with sandy plaster. No form of wall support (with possible exception of a metate set into wall); walls slump badly 1 ft. above floor.

Floor: Thin layer of adobe clay over sterile soil. Depth 7 ft. 11 in. below surface.

Hearth(s): Circular, clay-lined basin, placed slightly nearer ventilator than rear wall (assuming truly circular shape). (Seven ft. 4 in. from hearth center to ventilator, 7 ft. 11 in. from hearth center to wall at right angle to hearth-ventilator axis, presumably 8 ft. 6 in. from hearth center to rear wall.) Encircled by clay coping 4 in. wide, 3 in. high. Interior diameter 1 ft. 11 in., depth 8 in. Indications of older hearth found; same construction and approximately same dimensions as above. Center *ca.* 5 in. southwest of later hearth's center; southwest portion of clay coping intact. Hearth(s) filled with white ash.

Ashpit: Area between hearth and ventilator badly soaked by rain during excavation. Subsequent examination revealed elliptic area of ash and stained earth, 2 ft. along hearth-ventilator axis, 11 in. wide, 8 in. deep. Presumably remains of ashpit; center 5 ft. 5 in. from ventilator opening.

Ladder-post sockets (?): Vestiges of two circular holes, 6 in. and 7 in. in diameter, traced to depth of 2.5 in. Placed symmetrically on opposite sides of hearth-ventilator axis, centers 1 ft. 2 in. apart.

Deflector or damper slab: Remains of sandstone slab on floor near ventilator; originally 1 ft. 5 in. by 1 ft. by 2 in. Shape rectangular with one short side rounded and beveled by grinding.

Ventilator: Southeast of hearth, opening consists of break in slumping wall 1 ft. 7 in. wide at floor level. Opening either oval or rectangular; ventilator passage not excavated.

Postholes: One located east of hearth, appropriate to four-post roof support system. Diameter 9 in., depth 8 in., distance from wall 2 ft. Rodent passage on northwest side terminates in bulbous end which may indicate another post; 9 in. diameter, 6 in. deep.

Floor features: Considerable amount of adobe on floor near wall south of ventilator. May have been a coping or bin, but seems doubtful. Investigation behind wall in this area completely negative.

Fill: Compact dirt containing charcoal and gravel to depth of 1 ft. 5 in. below surface; homogeneous charcoal-stained sand (apparently windblown) 1 ft. 5 in.-7 ft. 11 in. below surface, with adobe fragments numerous below 6 ft. 3 in.

Pits

Irregular unplastered pits were found throughout the dwelling area. Most of them were round, with diameters up to 2 ft. 6 in., and contained little besides stained fill. In one area (Trench 4) of approximately 30 sq. ft., containing the remnants of two (oval?) floors, eight of these unplastered pits were found. The significance of these features was not determined.

A single clay-lined pit was found in the southwestern portion of the dwelling area. It is 2 ft. 6 in. in diameter, its bottom 3 ft. 2 in. below surface, and its top was traced to within 2 ft. of ground level.

Trenches

·Several exploratory trench and floor numbers have been retained to designate find-spots. In many cases, these "floors" were not well-defined and appeared to have little, if any, architectural significance; some doubtlessly represent no more than buried occupation levels.

Trench 1 encompasses F II in what was later called the Intermediate Area. No material recovered from trench.

Trench 2 room area, west of large slab-based wall.

Trench 2E room area, east of large slab-based wall. Floor 1, 1 ft. below surface, associated with adobe wall; Floor 2, 2 ft. 11 in. below surface, associated with Feature A.

Trench 3 encompasses Feature C and area to north. Floor 1, 1 ft. 6 in. to 1 ft. 10 in. below surface, very doubtful; Floor 2, 3 ft. below surface, patches only.

Trench 4 room area, south of large slab-based wall. Floor 1, 1 ft. 10 in. below surface; Floor 2, 2 ft. 5 in. below surface.

Trench 5 original designation of kiva test.

Trench 6 encompasses Feature D. Floor 1, 1 ft. 7 in. to 1 ft. 11 in. below surface, very doubtful.

Trench 7 sterile test.

Trench 8 area north of Trench 3, east of Feature B.

POTTERY (see Figure 6)

The larger numbers of sherds in Area B come from Trenches 2E, 3, 8, and the kiva. Santa Fe B/W (Pl. V *a-k*) is the most common decorated ware; sherds classified as Kwahe'e B/W (Pl. V *l-m*) are very rare. Many of the painted sherds are not classified (Pl. V

	SURFACE	TRENCH 2E abv fl 1	TRENCH 2E blw fl 1	TRENCH 2E misc.	TRENCH 2E sum	TRENCH 3 abv fl 1	TRENCH 3 blw fl 1	TRENCH 3 misc.	TRENCH 3 sum	TRENCH 8	TRENCH 4 abv fl 1	TRENCH 4 blw fl 1	TRENCH 4 misc.	TRENCH 4 sum	TRENCH 6 abv fl 1	TRENCH 6 blw fl 1	TRENCH 6 misc.	TRENCH 6 sum	TRENCH 2	KIVA upper fill	KIVA lower fill	KIVA misc fill	KIVA floor	KIVA sum	AREA B TOTAL
SANTA FE B/W	15	1		7	8	38	3	7	48	8			1	1	4			4	1					0	85
SANTA FE B/W ?	1				0		1	1	2	1				0				0	1					0	5
KWAHE'E B/W ?	1				0	1			1	0				0				0	0	1				1	3
RED MESA B/W	0		1		1			1	1	1			1	1				0	0				3	3	7
RED MESA B/W ?	1				0	1			1	2				0			1	1	2				2	2	9
FINE PASTE GRAY	1				0	6	1		7	7			1	1				0	0			2		2	18
COARSE PASTE GRAY	3			3	3	5		2	7	3			2	2	1	1	1	3	1	2	2	2	1	7	29
TRADE AND INTRUSIVE	0			2	2	3			3	0			1	1				0	1					0	7
BISCUIT B ?	0				0	1			1	0				0				0	0					0	1
UNIDENTIFIED B/W	8			2	2	11	1	3	15	8	3		1	4				0	2	1	2		2	5	44
POLISHED BROWN	2				0	2			2	0				0				0	0					0	4
sum	32	1	1	14	16	68	6	14	88	30	3	0	7	10	5	1	2	8	8	4	4	4	8	20	212
CORRUGATED	1				0	2			2	0	1			1				0	0	1		1		2	6
NECK-BANDED	24	1	4	24	29	28	7	5	40	15	8		4	12	3	4	2	9	17	6	1	11	8	26	172
NECK-RIBBED	1				0	1			1	4				0				0	0	1		1		2	8
SMEARED-INDENTED	3	1	2	3	6	41	6	47	94	3	1		2	3				0	5					0	114
PUNCTATE	0				0	1			1	0				0				0	0					0	1
SCORED	0				0				0	0				0				0	0		2	1		3	3
HANDLES	0				0	3	1	1	5	1				0				0	1					0	7
sum	29	2	6	27	35	76	14	53	143	23	10	0	6	16	3	4	2	9	23	8	3	14	8	33	311
PLAIN SURFACE	60	20	14	26	60	46	15	18	79	32	10	0	2	12	1	3	0	4	25	14	10	13	11	48	320
SUM (total)	121	23	21	67	111	190	35	85	310	85	23	0	15	38	9	8	4	21	56	26	17	31	27	101	843

Figure 6 – Provenience of potsherds, Area B.

s-y); these are discussed in a later section. Red Mesa B/W (Pl. V *o-r*), possibly Biscuit B. (Pl. V *n*), and Kwahe'e B/W occur in addition to the Santa Fe and unidentified B/W sherds.

Painted Sherds

Santa Fe B/W (Pl. V a-k*):* Distribution shown in Figure 13; see also Mera, 1935; Stubbs and Stallings, 1953; Wendorf 1953. These sherds conform to published descriptions of the type. The paste used is the same as that described for Kwahe'e B/W in Area A. Of the 85 sherds recovered, 62 (73 per cent) show no temper or only occasional inclusions of mica and/or bits or rock. Twelve sherds (14 per cent) may have been tempered sparsely with finely crushed sherd; an equal number may have been sand-tempered. Of the sherds which may contain sand temper, only one is definitely sand-tempered. The others contain occasional large quartz grains in the paste. None of the sherds was tempered with crushed rock.

Seven bowl sherds (8 per cent) have exterior slip; three of these are rim sherds. Eight bowl sherds (from four vessels?) have basket-impressed exteriors. The basketry represented is fairly uniform: eleven stitches and 5.5 to 6.0 coils to the inch (Pl. V k). The stitch impressions on the sherd exteriors slant upward to the left.

Of the eighteen rim sherds recovered, sixteen were from bowls. (See Figure 7 *a-d*.) Of the latter, ten lips were slipped, three painted.

Seventy-nine sherds (93 per cent) are painted on the interior and presumably represent bowls. Three sherds may be from ollas, two are from canteens or small jars, and one is from a small seed jar. No whole or reconstructable vessels were recovered.

Red Mesa B/W (Pl. V o-r*):* The Red Mesa B/W from Area B is similar to that from Area A. The seven sherds of Red Mesa B/W appear to be of nonlocal paste, with sherd temper predominant. These few sherds represent jars, ollas, ladles and bowls. An additional nine sherds are classified as Red Mesa ? B/W; four are of nonlocal paste, three are of local paste, and two are indeterminate.

No sherds are classified as Gallup B/W.

Unidentified B/W (Pl. V s-y*):* In many cases it is difficult to place these sherds into categories of local and nonlocal paste. Such a difficulty was not encountered in Area A. Nine of these sherds are quite probably of fine local paste, with small amounts of sherd and/or rock temper added. Nineteen sherds are apparently of coarser nonlocal paste. I cannot place sixteen specimens in either

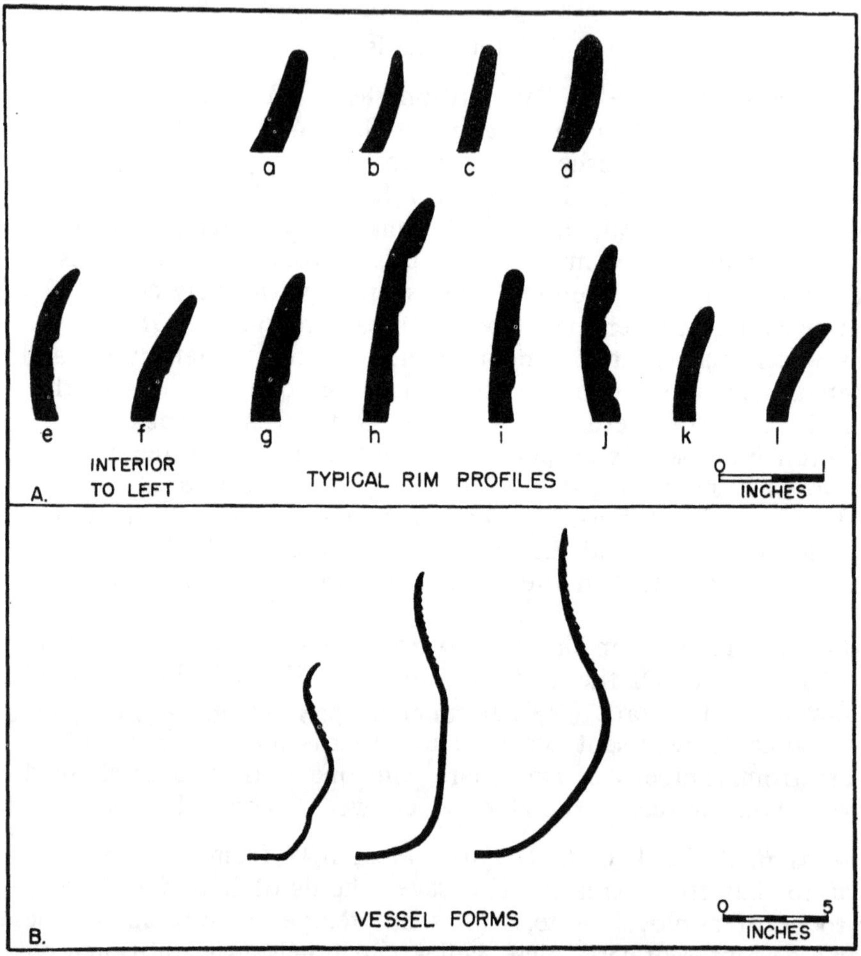

Figure 7–A. Typical rim profiles, Area B: *a-d*, Santa Fe B/W; *e*, corrugated; *f-i*, neck-banded, *j*, neck-ribbed; *k-l*, plain surface.
B. Vessel forms, Area B: all neck-banded.

class with any assurance.

All of these sherds are decorated with mineral paint. Decoration of all jar sherds and all but seven of the bowl sherds is executed in a fairly heavy-lined technique which is more similar to Kwahe'e than Red Mesa decoration. There are five examples of curvilinear decoration in this group.

Thirty of these sherds are presumably from bowls, eleven from jars, two from ladles, and one is from a handle. Of the bowl sherds, all but two rim fragments have an exterior slip; many are heavily slipped. All but one of the body sherds have exterior slip. At least five of the bowl rim sherds have painted lips.

Six of the bowl rim sherds and nine of the bowl body sherds are decorated in what can be considered as a somewhat aberant Kwahe'e B/W style, with sherd temper and exterior slip (e.g. Pl. V *t, v*). This conforms to Mera's description of Taos B/W and these sherds are probably of this pottery type. The jar, handle (Pl. V *x*), and ladle sherds can also be placed in this category.

Two bowl rim sherds (Pl. V *u, y*) and five bowl body sherds appear to be rather crude local imitations of Red Mesa B/W. The remaining sherds cannot be placed in even these tenuous categories.

The reader should be cautioned that the above remarks concerning similarities to Kwahe'e, Taos, and Red Mesa B/W are offered primarily as descriptive notes and are not definite type indentifications.

Unpainted Sherds

Unpainted Gray Sherds; non-culinary: The unpainted gray-ware sherds have been divided into fine paste gray (local?) and coarser paste gray (nonlocal?) as before. Two rim sherds of fine paste and one of coarser paste were recovered. The distinction between the fine and coarse paste is not as pronounced in Area B as it is in Area A. Only those sherds which could be considered as unpainted fragments of Santa Fe or Kwahe'e B/W are classified as "fine paste gray."

Other Unpainted Sherds; culinary: The great majority of the culinary sherds are either neck-banded, smeared-indented, or plain-surfaced. All of these classes of pottery seem to have been made from the local culinary paste described for Area A. All sherds discussed below are of this paste unless noted otherwise.

Neck-banded (Figure 7 f-i; *Pl. VI* a-g*):* All rim and side sherds, no bases. There are also two complete vessels (Pl. VIII *c-d*). Both have slightly flaring necks, lack shoulders, and have plain-surfaced lower bodies (Trench 2E, floor 1). One base is flat, one subconical. Of the 172 sherds, 25 are rims. These neck-banded sherds are similar to those from Area A, and the same methods of treating the coils were observed. Bands are .4 to .5 in. (10.4-12.7 mm.) wide. Thirty-three sherds (including nine rim sherds) have unmodified coils (Pl. VI *a-b*). Sixty-five sherds (including eight rim sherds) have beveled bands (Pl. VI *c*). Sixty-eight sherds (including seven rim sherds) have been beveled and/or smoothed to such an extent that the coil lines are obliterated (Pl. VI *d-e*). Six sherds (including one rim sherd) are "banded incised" (Pl. VI *f-g*).

In addition, there is one neck-banded sherd of nonlocal paste with sand temper (Pl. VI *m*). This appears to be typical Kana-a, and is classified as a trade sherd.

Smeared-indented (Pl. VI h-i*):* These sherds are quite similar to the Tesuque Smeared-indented described by Mera (1935:14). The surface treatment of many sherds, however, resembles that of Cundiyo Micaceous-indented and also that of the culinary ware shown accompanying Gallisteo B/W (see Mera, 1935: Pl. XI). Actually there is a transition in surface treatment from highly irregular to fairly regular indentations. In some cases it is difficult to decide whether a sherd is shallowly indented and well smeared, or just poorly smoothed plain-surfaced ware.

Miscellaneous Culinary; surface altered. Corrugated: Six sherds, including one rim sherd (Figure 7 *e*; Pl. VI 1) All corrugations are deep and evenly spaced. These sherds represent the sub-type observed in Area A. In addition, there is a single corrugated sherd of nonlocal paste (gray) with sherd and crushed quartz temper which has a white slip over the corrugations (Pl. VI *n*). This specimen is probably intrusive.

Neck-ribbed: Eight sherds, no rims (Figure 7 *j*; Pl. VI *j*). All ribs apparently emphasized by incision. Three or four vessels represented. Five sherds have ribs .20 to .25 in. (5.1-6.4 mm.) wide, and measure *ca.* .10 in. (2.5 mm.) from coil juncture to rib surface. Another sherd is similar to these, but shows deep (*ca.* .13 in. or 3.3 mm.) corrugation on a small part of its surface (Pl. VI *k*). Two sherds have ribs .27 to .30 in. (6.8-7.6 mm.) wide and measure *ca.* .15 in. (3.8 mm.) from coil juncture to rib surface.

Punctate: One body sherd. Shallow ovate punctations made with a stick or possibly a finger. It was too small to determine whether or not a pattern was formed.

Scored: Three body sherds, probably from two vessels. Two sherds (from one vessel) are fairly thick and are scored on both interior and exterior. The third sherd is scored on the exterior only (Pl. VI *o*).

Plain surface: Three hundred twenty sherds of plain-surfaced culinary ware, made from local paste, were recovered. Twelve of these were rim sherds (Figure 7 *k-l*), another thirteen were from bases of vessels. Other sherds were quite small, and permit few generalizations concerning vessel shape. No sherds indicating pronounced shoulders were found. No complete or restorable vessels were recovered. The plain-surfaced ware from Area B appears similar to that from Area A; the ware from Area B may be slightly thicker, but no pronounced difference is involved.

These sherds represent plain-surfaced vessels, the lower portions of neck-banded, ribbed, corrugated, punctate, and, less probably, smeared-indented vessels. None of the twelve rim sherds recovered are large enough to indicate that they are from vessels whose entire exterior surface is plain. These rim sherds show straight and everted lips, similar to those for other types of culinary pottery. Basal sherds indicate both flat and rounded-bottom vessels.

Miscellaneous Culinary; Plain Surface. Brownware: Four body sherds of nonlocal paste. These sherds are fairly well polished, with core color black to brown. Crushed rock temper has been added liberally. Thickness varies from .15 to .20 in. (3.8-5.1 mm.). One sherd shows red slip on its concave surface. These sherds may be from four different vessels.

Other: A thick (.40-.65 in. or 10.4-16.4 mm.), roughly circular sherd *ca.* 1.8 in. (45.7 mm.) in diameter, from the kiva fill. One surface is convex and smooth, the other concave and rough. This may be from the base of a hand-modelled vessel.

Handles: As is the case with the plain-surfaced sherds described above, it is difficult to ascribe these specimens to any particular type of vessel (i.e., neck-banded, plain-surfaced, etc.). Seven whole or fragmentary handles were recovered. Four were strap handles, two were two-rope handles, and one is too fragmentary to classify.

Three of the strap handles are fairly large (Pl. VI *p-q*). Their maximum dimensions vary from 2.25 to 2.50 in. (57.2-63.5 mm.)

plus, their width is *ca.* 1 in. (25.4 mm.). The smaller strap handle has a maximum outside dimension of 1.10 in. (27.9 mm.) and is .60 in. (15.2 mm.) wide (Pl. VI *r*). It is of local culinary paste, but has a white slip on its exterior surface.

The two-rope handles are of approximately the same size, with maximum exterior dimensions *ca.* 1.40 in. (35.8 mm.), width .65 in. (16.4 mm.). One is complete. It was attached horizontally, and may be a strap handle with a medial incision rather than a true two-coil handle. The other specimen is fragmentary, but is definitely a two-coil handle (Pl. VI *t*). Its method of attachment cannot be ascertained.

The unidentified specimen is a body sherd showing a fragmentary stub of a "nubbin," strap, or loop handle, .50 in. (12.7 mm.) in diameter.

Artifacts; ceramic

Scrapers: Five sherds with one edge smoothed. One with a smooth concave edge (coarse paste, gray; Pl. VI *y*); one with a smooth convex edge (coarse paste, gray; Pl. VI *x*); one small fragment smoothed on one edge and rounded at a corner (Santa Fe B/W; Pl. VI *u*); two fragments with a smooth straight edge (Unidentified B/W; Pl. VI *w*; and Santa Fe B/W; Pl. VI *v*).

Pipe: Trench 2E, below floor 1 (Pl. VI *z*). Probably associated with one of pit structures. Short slender cloud-blower. Fine culinary paste, smoothed, undecorated. Length 1.65 in. Outside diameter: bit .30 in., bowl .55 in. Interior bowl diameter .40 in., depth of bowl .65 in. No signs of use.

ARTIFACTS OF STONE

Projectile Points (Pl. VII *a-k*)

Only notched and/or stemmed forms are discussed in this category. Descriptive details are given in Table 4.

Eleven whole or fragmentary projectile points were recovered. All are corner-notched. With but two exceptions (Pl. VII *j-k*), all are small (length .54-*ca.* 1.07 in., median .81 in.; width .35 to .61 in., median .47 in.). All but four of the specimens are of obsidian. The majority have expanding stems, others are straight. Blade edges are usually straight or slightly convex; three points have serrated blades. The two larger points, both from the kiva, could be classified as knives.

TABLE 4
PROJECTILE POINT DIMENSIONS, AREA B
(In Inches)

Reference Plate VII	NOTCHES		STEM			BLADE EDGE			LENGTH	WIDTH	THICKNESS	MATERIAL	LOCUS
	COR.	SIDE	EXP.	STR.	CONT.	CONV.	STR.	CONC.					
j	x	. . .	x	. . .	. . .	x	. . .	. . .	(3.00)	1.36	.24	Obsd.	Kiva, floor
k	x	. . .	x	. . .	. . .	x	x	. . .	1.50	(1.10)	.24	Chal.	Kiva, floor
c	x?	. . .	?	?	?	. . .	. . .	sxs	(1.07)	.61	.11	Chert	Tr. 2
f	x	. . .	x	. . .	. . .	x	x	. . .	(1.00)	.54	.13	Chal.	Surface
b	x	. . .	x	. . .	. . .	x	xs	. . .	.95	.44	.10	Obsd.	Tr. 2E, fl. 1
a	x	. . .	x	. . .	. . .	x	. . .	. . .	(.82)	.45	.12	Obsd.	Tr. 2E, fl. 1
d	x	. . .	. . .	x	. . .	x	x	. . .	.81	.51	.15	Obsd.	Tr. 2
e	x?	. . .	?	?	?	. . .	sxs	. . .	(.80)	.55	.10	Obsd.	Tr. 2
g	x	. . .	x	. . .	. . .	x	. . .	. . .	.76	.45	.10	Obsd.	Surface
h	x	. . .	?	?	. . .	. . .	x	. . .	(.63)	(.47)	.10	Chal.	Surface
i	x	. . .	. . .	x	. . .	. . .	x	. . .	.54	.35	.08	Obsd.	Surface

x = present
xs = present, one edge serrate
sxs = present, both edges serrate
(-) = estimated dimension

TABLE 5
LOCUS OF CHIPPED STONE ARTIFACTS, AREA B

LOCUS/CLASS	A	B	B'	C	D	E	F	TOTALS
Surface	7	0	1	0	0	0	2	10
Tr. 2E abv. fl. 1 . . .	0	0	0	1	4	0	0	5
Tr. 2E blw. fl. 1 . . .	9	1	1	0	2	0	1	14
Tr. 2E misc.	4	1	2	2	7	1	0	17
Tr. 3 abv. fl. 1	0	0	3	0	0	1	0	4
Tr. 3 blw. fl. 1	0	0	0	0	0	0	0	0
TR. 3 misc..	0	0	0	0	0	0	0	0
Tr. 8	0	0	0	1	0	1	0	2
Tr. 4 abv. fl. 1	0	0	0	0	7	0	1	8
Tr. 4 blw. fl. 1	0	0	0	0	1	1	0	2
Tr. 4 misc.	0	0	0	0	3	0	0	3
Tr. 6 abv. fl. 1	1	0	0	0	0	0	0	1
Tr. 6 blw. fl. 1	1	0	0	0	0	0	1	2
Tr. 6 misc.	0	0	0	0	0	0	0	0
Tr. 2	8	0	1	0	1	1	0	11
Kiva, upper fill	0	0	0	0	0	0	0	0
Kiva, lower fill	0	0	0	0	0	0	0	0
Kiva, misc. fill	0	0	0	0	0	0	0	0
Kiva, floor	0	0	0	0	0	0	0	0
Totals	30	2	8	4	25	5	5	79

Other Chipped Stone (see Table 5 for locus)

Class A: (Flakes showing retouch or use; unshaped) thirty specimens. All are apparently flakes (two possible exceptions). All are retouched or show use flakes on one side only. Eight examples have steep retouch; with but one exception, these specimens are from fairly large and/or thick flakes. In this respect they differ from the analogous specimens found in Area A. Eighteen are fairly thick flakes with one or more thin edges showing retouch or use. There are three small, thin, apparently random flakes showing use. One specimen has roughly parallel sides with use or retouch along these edges, and could be called a blade.

Five specimens show use or retouch along a concave edge. Six of the flakes with thick retouched edges may be end scrapers.

Class B: (Flakes retouched and shaped, not pointed; Pl. VII *l-m*) two specimens. Small bifacially flaked pieces of obsidian. Both may be points or knives with broken tips. Retouch and/or use indicated along all other edges.

Class B': (Flakes shaped and retouched to a point; Pl. VII *n-u*) nine specimens. One thick, roughly triangular specimen, with use and/or retouch along all edges. Seven smaller triangular specimens, bifacially retouched.

Class C: (Unretouched flakes, jagged edge) four specimens. All fairly large. Three have jagged edges that are quite thin. No indications of use, but are suitable for cutting.

Class D: (Random flakes; edges smooth, not sharply pointed, no retouch) twenty-five specimens.

Class E: (Sharply pointed random flakes, no retouch) five specimens. These flakes are of the same sizes as those of category B' and would have been included therein if they had showed any signs of use.

Class F: (Cores, or possibly thick heavily-chipped flakes) five specimens. Four smaller specimens, none with any dimension greater than 2.2 in. One of these is very small, and may be only a fragment from a thick unworked flake. One larger specimen, roughly square, has one convex face; the other face is flat and shows flake scars. 2.3 by 2.5 by 1.3 in. maximum thickness.

Metates and Manos

Trough metates:

1) Kiva fill: Small fragment of trough metate, closed at one end. Not possible to estimate original dimensions.

2) Kiva wall: Fragment of trough metate, closed at one end. No measurements recorded.

3-5) Three small fragments of what appear to have been trough metates closed at one end, recovered in the dwelling area. None were of sufficient size to estimate original dimensions. These fragments were found: (3) Trench 2; (4) Trench 2E, floor 2; (5) Trench 6 (Feature D).

Manos:

1) Surface: Oval mano, 5 by 5 by 2 in. One surface smooth.

2-3) Kiva, fill: Two oval manos, 5.5 by 5 by 2 in. and 5.5 by 5 by 1.5 in. (lava). Both have one smooth surface.

4-5) Trench 1: Two oval manos, 6 by 4 by 2 in. and 5 by 4 by 2 in. Former has one smooth surface, latter has two.

6) Trench 2: Oval mano, 5.5 by 4 by 2 in. One smooth surface.

7-8) Trench 2E, Floor 1: Two oval manos, 8 by 5 by 1.5 in. and 8.5 by 5 by 3 in. Both have two smooth surfaces. Latter has smooth indentations or (finger?) grooves in longer sides.

9) Trench 2E, Floor 1: Rectangular mano with rounded corners; 7 by 4.5 by 1 in. Two smooth surfaces.

10) Trench 2E, below Floor 1: Oval mano, 5 by 4 by 2 in. One side slightly convex, well smoothed.

11-12) Trench 2E, Floor 2: Two oval manos, 5 by 4 by 1.8 in. and 7 by 4 by 2 in. No data with regard to number of smooth surfaces.

13-14) Trench 2E, indeterminate (probably fill of Feature A): Two thick rounded manos or "floor polishers"; 6 by 5 by 3 in. and 5 by 4.5 by 2 in. Former shows much use on one flat face, latter shows slight use on one slightly convex face.

17-18) Trench 4, indeterminate, floor 2 or below: One oval mano, 6 by 4 by 2 in. with one surface worn and other surface pecked. Other specimen, 5 by 4 by 3 in. shows little wear, and may be no more than a smooth rounded river boulder.

Axes, Mauls, and Hammerstones

Axes and Mauls: none recovered.

Hammerstones:

A. Trench 2E: Round, flat specimen showing much battering, also removal of large flakes. Diameters 2.4 to 2.8 in., maximum thickness 1.2 in. Could be considered as a core or a crude chopper.

B. Trench 4: Flattened ellipsoidal stone, maximum diameter 2.7 in., maximum cross section diameter 2.2 in. Shows battering or pecking.

C. Trench 4: Nearly spherical stone, battered. Diameters 2.3 to 2.6 in.

Miscellaneous Smoothed Stone:

A. Trench 2: Broken piece of green stone 2.3 in. wide and .5 in. thick which seems to have been used as a whetstone, grinder or polisher.

B. Trench 3: Turquoise pendant (Pl. VII *w*). Roughly rectangular with rounded edges. Edges smooth but specimen not symmetrical due to irregular shape of base. Very thin. .45 in. maximum height, .40 in. wide, .04 in. maximum thickness. Hole .05 in. diameter, drilled from both sides.

ARTIFACTS OF BONE

Awls or Flakers

All ten examples apparently made from mammal leg-bone.

Class A: head of bone intact, no specimens.

Class B: head of bone unaltered except for original splitting, five specimens; two from Tr. 2E (Pl. VII *x* and *ee*), Tr. 4 (Pl. VII *bb*), Kiva lower fill (Pl. VII *z*), Kiva floor (Pl. VII *aa*).

Class C: head partly worked down, two specimens; Tr. 2E (Pl. VII *y*), Tr. 4 (Pl. VII *cc*).

Classes D, E: head entirely removed or made from splinters, no specimens.

Class F: unidentified, three specimens; all Tr. 2E (Pl. VII *dd, ff-gg*). Distal fragments with heads missing.

Short bone tube (bead?): (Tr. 2E; Pl. VII *ii*). Cut section of bone from a large bird, possibly turkey. Length 1.25 in., diameter .43 to .36 in. Cuts are not smoothed.

Split and cut deer metapodial: (Tr. 4; Pl. VII *jj*). Split longitudinally and distal portion cut off. Cut made by wide groove. Not smoothed across cut, but beveled somewhat. Not smoothed across split. 7.35 in. in length, maximum width 1.12 in., .45 in. thick. Use conjectural, no indication of having been used as a scraper.

Cut bird bone; from turkey or eagle: (Tr. 3; Pl. VII *hh*). 3.46 in. long, diameter .56-.41 in. No other indication of having been worked.

ARTIFACTS OF SHELL

One specimen, recovered from Trench 2E (Pl. VII *ν*). Worked to a rectangular shape, but not drilled. .71 by .40 by .06 in. thick.

INTERMEDIATE AREA

It has been noted that the two areas in which sherds and architectural remnants occurred were separated by some 475 feet. Exploratory trenches revealed two isolated features between these areas. The first of these was found some 150 feet southeast of Area A. The second feature, more poorly defined, was about 400 feet southeast of Area A, and about 75 feet northwest of Area B (see Figure 1). These two features, called Feature I and Feature II respectively, are described separately because their location and the material associated with them do not indicate that they are extensions of either Area A or Area B.

Immediately southeast of, and slightly uphill from, Feature I a surface concentration of gravel was found. It was roughly square, about twelve feet across. This gravel concentration, upon testing, appeared to contain no signs of human activity. It was about 2 ft. 2 in. thick, and rested on the same yellow sterile soil into which Feature I was excavated.

FEATURE I: (FIGURE 8, UPPER LEFT)

Feature I was an irregularly-shaped floor area, roughly elliptical with diameters of 21 ft. and 13 ft. 6 in. The floor was located beneath the slope of a small knoll, and its depth below surface varied from 10 in. to 3 ft. The floor and "walls" were demarcated only by a sterile zone inside which charcoal-stained fill was found. In this floor area many pits had been dug, the largest of which was elliptical, with diameters of 2 ft. 8 in. by 3 ft. 11 in., and which reached a depth below floor level of 1 ft. 11 in.

No well-defined roof support system was found, but an arrangement of peripheral posts may have existed. A burned area in the middle of the floor suggests a hearth, but no depression, hearth coping, or ash concentration was found.

The fill of Feature I was gravelly, charcoal-stained sand. The floor was marked in places by a slightly compacted layer of charcoal-stained sand; more often it was defined by uncovering the sterile substratum of sand and gravel.

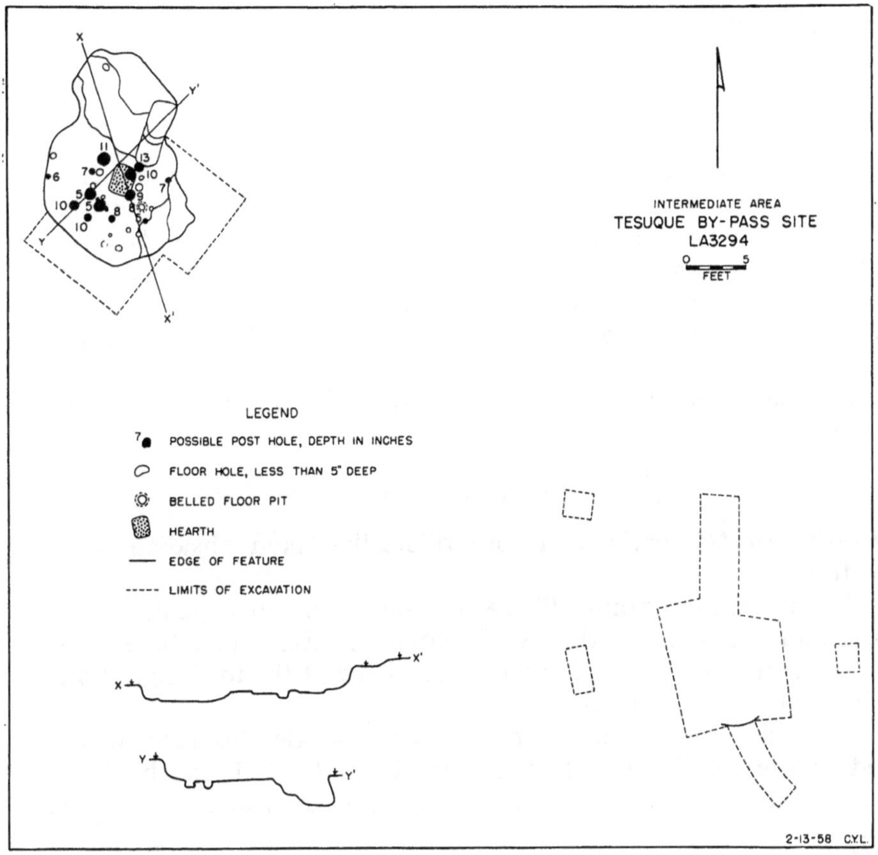
INTERMEDIATE AREA
TESUQUE BY-PASS SITE
LA3294
0 5
FEET
LEGEND
POSSIBLE POST HOLE, DEPTH IN INCHES
FLOOR HOLE, LESS THAN 5" DEEP
BELLED FLOOR PIT
HEARTH
EDGE OF FEATURE
LIMITS OF EXCAVATION
X
X'
Y
Y'
2-13-58 C.Y.L.

Figure 8

Artifacts recovered from the fill and floor were kept separate in most cases; some finds are described herein as "indeterminate." These are probably, but not positively, from the fill. The artifacts and other indications of human activity are listed below.

Pottery

Seven sherds of unpainted ware, probably from three different vessels. Six are from the fill, one from the floor. All sherds are probably from vessels with altered surfaces; two sherds from the fill are too small for positive identification, but appear to be bits of a larger sherd which has a corrugated surface. Two sherds (one fill, one floor) show neck-banding, three (fill) show slight corrugation.

One small painted sherd (unidentified B/W) was found near the floor.

Stone Artifacts

Projectile points: Portions of four bifacially-flaked obsidian points were found.

A fragmentary point (Pl. IX *b*) was found in a posthole. It is thin and triangular with slightly concave edges. The basal portion is missing. Probably corner-notched, *ca.* 1.00 in. long, about .55 in. wide, .11 in. thick.

A small, thin, triangular point with a single shoulder, was found in the fill (Pl. IX *a*). The stem is contracted, the blade edges slightly convex. It is .72 in. long, .46 in. wide, and .09 in. thick.

From indeterminate locations in Feature I (probably fill) two other points were recovered. One is a small, thin, triangular point .75 in. long, .50 in. wide, and .10 in. thick, with small corner-notches (Pl. IX *d*.). The stem is contracted; one blade edge is slightly convex and the other is straight. The other point is long, thin, and triangular; 1.04 in. long, .55 in. wide, and .11 in. thick (Pl. IX *c*). Blade edges are slightly concave; it has two corner-notches and an expanding stem. The portion of this point which corresponds to the fragmentary point from the posthole is almost identical to it in all dimensions.

Other chipped stone: Sixteen pieces of stone, at least thirteen of them flakes, showed secondary flaking. Twelve were from the floor, three from the fill, and one is from an indeterminate postion. All but six pieces of retouched stone may be classed as "random flake scrapers": small flakes, evidently unshaped, which show signs of use or slight retouch at one or more points along an edge. The six pieces not so classified are described below.

A long petal-shaped flake of quartzite with a triangular cross section was recovered from the floor. It was 3.8 by 1.5 by .6 in. maximum thickness. One long edge shows signs of use. This object may have been used with a sawing motion.

Another relatively large flake with a triangular cross section was recovered from the floor. It shows retouch about a point. It measures 2.7 by 1.6 by .7 in. maximum thickness.

From the posthole containing the obsidian point there was also recovered a trapezoidal flake with one point carefully retouched and a well-made end scraper (Pl. IX *e*). The former measures 1.0 in. and .5 in. along its parallel sides, and has an altitude of .8 in. The latter is 1.3 in. long, 1.2 in. wide and .3 in. thick.

From the fill, a small triangular flake was recovered which may be retouched about one point. It measures 1.2 by .7 by .3 in.

An oval flake scraper, of indeterminate provenience, was found which shows use or retouch along one edge. It is 2.1 by 1.8 by .7 in. thick.

Unworked flakes: Twelve unworked flakes were found; ten at floor level, one in the fill, and one of indeterminate locus.

Miscellaneous Stone Artifacts. Manos (4) One was found in an unlined floor pit. It is 10.2 by 3.8 by 2.8 in. thick, rectangular with rounded ends. One end shows battering. One surface pecked. Granite.

A second mano, from the fill, tends to be round in horizontal section, 4.6 by 4.3 by 2.1 in. thick. One surface shows pecking. Granite.

The third mano, locus indeterminate, is oval, 4.6 by 3.7 by 2.5 in. thick. One (rounded) surface shows some use.

The fourth mano, locus indeterminate, is fragmentary. It appears to have been oval, with a wedge-shaped cross section. One surface is smoothed and flat. It is 3.7 by 4 by 1.5 in. thick; of granite.

Hammerstones (3): They are roughly spherical and show excessive battering. One (3.2 by 2.0 by 2.4 in.) is from the floor, one (2.5 by 2.1 by 1.8 in.) is from the fill, one (2.1 by 1.9 by 1.8 in.) is from an indeterminate location.

Unworked boulders (4): One is smooth and fairly spherical, with an average diameter of *ca.* 2.8 in. One smooth boulder, roughly rectangular, may have been used as a floor polisher. It measures 4.0 by 3.5 by 2.4 in. One fractured and weathered boulder measures 4.3 by 3.0 by 2.2 in. All three of the above were found on the floor of Feature I. A fourth boulder, from an indeterminate location, is roughly ovate, measuring 4.4 by 4.5 by 3.0 in.

Pebbles (3): All had rectangular cross sections with rounded corners. They are from 2.6 to 3.0 in. long, 1.1 to 1.2 in. wide, and .6 to .9 in. thick. Two are from the floor, the third is from the fill. One of the pebbles from the floor is of quartzite and is quite smooth. It may have been used as a polishing stone. The other two pebbles have fairly rough surfaces and show no signs of use.

Bone Artifacts

A piece of bone appears to have been used as an awl or gouge. The point, however, is not well smoothed, and may only be the result of an accidental break.

A section of antelope horn-core, 4.6 in. long, has a point which is rounded and smooth, but not polished (Pl. IX *g*). Half of the shaft is split away from the proximal portion, for a distance of 2.4 in. There is a suggestion of smoothing at the proximal end, but the rest of the cut is jagged. At several places there are small parallel scratches which give the impression that the horn-core had been worked with a stone flake.

FEATURE II (FIGURE 8)

Feature II was a poorly defined floor area, demarcated only by a change from the stained fill to the sterile ground. It was partially excavated. No pits were found in the floor area, and no fire area was discovered. In one sector a suggestion of a small portion of wall occurred; it was *ca.* 3 ft. in length and less than a foot high. The "floor" occurred at a depth of 1 ft. 4 in. The fill was homogeneous of charcoal-stained sand and gravel. No separation of artifacts found in the fill and near floor level was made. Artifacts recovered are described below.

Pottery

Eleven sherds were found. None are painted but two show traces of slip. The slipped sherds and five others do not have altered surfaces. Of the four remaining sherds, one shows banding and two show corrugation of fairly narrow coils. The fourth shows a series of light linear incisions which seem to follow a pattern. There are three parallel incisions down the middle of the sherd, spaced about .19 in. (4.8 mm.) apart. Pendant from one of the outer lines is a series of oblique incisions, also parallel, and *ca.* .15 in. (3.8 mm.) apart. The design produced, then, is oblique hatchure pendant from parallel lines.

Stone Artifacts

Twenty flakes were recovered, ten show signs of retouch or use. Two show retouch about a point, two are fragments of blades with use flakes along one edge, six are random flake scrapers.
Manos: (4) One is rectangular with rounded corners, 4.9 by 3.65 by 1.8 in. thick. Two surfaces show wear. One end shows slight battering. A second mano, rectangular with rounded corners, is 6.0 by 4.0 by 1.4 in. thick. One surface shows wear and one end shows slight battering. The third mano is circular, 4.4 in. in diameter and 2.3 in. thick. One surface shows wear from a circular motion. The fourth mano is fragmentary, oval or rectangular, with steeply rounded corners. It measures ? by 4 by 2.9 in. thick. One surface shows slight signs of use. The edges of the break have a smooth bevel in spots.
Other artifacts: A smooth flat bouider was found. It is trapezoidal with smoothly rounded corners. The only suggestion of use is a small nick taken out of the top. The parallel sides are 5.0 in. and 2.5 in., the altitude is 4.9 in., thickness 1.7 in.

Bone Artifacts

A bone needle or bodkin, made from an unidentified mammal long-bone (Pl. IX *g*). Complete except for small fragment of tip. Shaft 5.03 in. long, .34 in. wide, .16 in. thick, with edges rounded. One end drilled from both sides, diameter of "eye" .08 in. Scratches run diagonally across this end of the specimen, and the shaft is slightly thinned at this point. The other end is spatulate; width .5 in. from tip is .28 in., thickness .07 in. Edges are worn quite sharp for a distance of 1.0 in. from tip.

SITE ANALYSIS AND INTERPRETATION

Excavations at the Tesuque By-Pass Site disclosed two major and one intermediate occupation areas. Analysis of architecture and artifacts indicates at least four temporally separate occupations (components) at the site; possibly there were more.

Paucity of artifacts and complex relationships between fragmentary architectural features preclude a straightforward interpretation of the cultural components represented, and a comment on the analytic approach adopted will be pertinent. An initial analysis dealing only with architecture and ceramic associations was made. Next all architectural features associated with a specific ceramic assemblage were grouped and interpreted as an "architectural-ceramic" complex, named for the predominant painted pottery type concerned. Some architectural features were "lost" to the indeterminate category at this point. Finally, associated non-ceramic artifacts were added to their appropriate complex to provide a basis for component definitions. Inevitably, some artifacts could not be assigned to a particular complex; no appeal was made to comparative (extra-site) data to remedy this situation.

Such an analysis, presented at length in the original thesis, must involve repetition of certain discrete associations and consideration of various alternative interpretations. An attempt has been made to eliminate some of these analytic niceties prior to publication; the paragraphs below emphasize associations most pertinent to that interpretation of the site which appears most reasonable.

AREA A

The room-block in Area A is apparently an architectural unit, and there is no structural evidence to indicate that some rooms are appreciably later than others. The room floors were shallowly buried and subfloor pits produced very little cultural material. Excavations designated Trench 1 and Trench 2 are shallow tests in the room-block area, and material from these two features was, in general, more shallowly buried than material found in the fill of the various rooms.

The ceramic assemblage associated with the room-block (see Figure 3) is characterized by a low percentage of painted sherds, with Kwahe'e B/W the most common decorated type. Vessels of Red Mesa and other black-on-white types are also present. Culinary vessels are represented primarily by plain, corrugated, and neck-banded (or -ribbed) sherds. Plain sherds, most of which probably represent lower portions of corrugated and neck-banded vessels, are the most common class, while corrugated sherds greatly outnumber neck-banded and neck-ribbed specimens.

The kiva in Area A is set within the right angle of the L-shaped room-block, and the resulting combination of room-block and kiva forms a standard unit of Pueblo architecture. Pottery found on the kiva floor, in the lower, and in the upper (I, II) levels of the kiva fill is similar to that found in the room-block.

The lower fill in the kiva contained little cultural debris, and the two feet of accumulated fill indicate that the kiva was not used as a trash pit immediately following its abandonment. There is nothing in the small pottery sample from the lower fill which indicates a ceramic complex that is markedly different from that of the upper kiva fill. There is a slightly higher proportion of neck-banded and neck-ribbed to corrugated sherds and a smaller percentage of painted sherds in the lower levels, but the number of specimens involved (Figure 3) is extremely small. Such differences as may exist are interpreted as indicative of temporal change rather than separate occupations of the site.

Apparently the kiva was used only by the earliest occupants of the room-block. When the kiva collapsed, the occupants continued to dispose of their trash in whatever manner they had used previously, and Levels III and IV of the kiva fill accumulated. Following this respectful interval, the partially filled structure was used as a trash dump by the room-block occupants. Judging by the slight changes in ceramics, this interval was not very long. Another kiva may have been constructed by the late occupants of the room-block, but no trace of it was found. The atypical, D-shaped room 5 may have served this purpose.

The only other architectural features found in Area A were four pits, located behind (i.e., northwest of) the room-block. No pottery was found in the pits, but their proximity to the room-block, the sherds found on the surface nearby, and the small pottery sample from Trench 4 (in the area of the pits) all suggest that the pits are associated with the room-block and kiva.

Hence, a single occupation of the Tesuque By-Pass Site appears to be represented in the architectural, ceramic, and consequently, the non-ceramic artifacts found in Area A. This occupation, defined in a later section, is designated as the "Kwahe'e Component."

AREA B

In Area B there was found a complicated jumble of fragmentary architectural features. The remains of several roundish structures, segments of adobe and slab-based walls, sections of floor, and a part of a semi-subterranean circular kiva were exposed.

In the ceramic collection from Area B, two classes of painted sherds are predominant: Santa Fe B/W and "unidentified B/W" (pp.33-35). Red Mesa B/W is present. Culinary vessels are represented primarily by plain surfaced, neck-banded, and smeared-indented sherds. Corrugated body sherds are conspicuous by their virtual absence (six sherds only). Although few sherds were found in any given feature, evidence was found throughout most of the site that the major ceramic groups were well mixed. This is in keeping with the nature of the architectural remains.

The kiva in Area B had not been used as a trash pit. Its fill was relatively homogeneous and contained but few sherds. No Santa Fe B/W or smeared-indented sherds were associated with this feature, but the kiva provides important evidence regarding the relationship of Red Mesa B/W and the unidentified B/W pottery. It is pertinent to recall the status of the latter ceramic group. It does not consist of a single unidentified B/W pottery type. Differences in design style, paste, and temper exist within this class, and more than one type is probably represented. On the other hand, these sherds have several attributes in common (pp. 33-35) and, as a class, show resemblances to both Red Mesa B/W and to the local variety of Kwahe'e B/W described for Area A. The apparent conformity of many of these specimens to Mera's description of Taos B/W (Mera, 1935: 5-6) has been noted.

Red Mesa B/W sherds were found only on the floor of the kiva, whereas other mineral-painted pottery (unidentified B/W) occurred both at floor level and throughout the fill. The unidentified B/W and the unpainted non-culinary sherds ("coarse paste gray," "fine paste gray") from floor level are, with one exception, of the coarser and presumably nonlocal paste. Bowl sherds are slipped on both exterior and interior surfaces. In these respects, the sherds resemble Red Mesa B/W. The exception noted above is of finer paste containing a small amount of sherd temper and is painted in a crude Red Mesa style of decoration.

Of the unidentified B/W and unpainted non-culinary sherds from the kiva fill, approximately equal quantities consist of coarser and finer paste. Sherds of the latter class contain small amounts of sherd or crushed rock temper, but in other respects their paste is similar to that of local Kwahe'e and Santa Fe B/W sherds. At least one unidentified sherd from the upper fill could be classified as nonlocal Kwahe'e B/W; one other sherd is probably local Kwahe'e. The few neck-banded sherds from the kiva were found throughout the fill, from just below present ground surface to floor level.

The pottery found on the kiva floor leaves little doubt that this structure was associated with a pre-Kwahe'e B/W occupation whose ceramic complex is characterized by nonlocal painted pottery, including Red Mesa B/W, and neck-banded culinary vessels. The differences observed in sherds from the kiva fill indicate a changing emphasis from nonlocal to local painted wares after the kiva was abandoned. Neck-banded culinary vessels remained in style; presumably these were made locally.

Circular Features A and B and the wall remnants found above them require careful consideration. This is the most complex architectural assemblage in Area B and its proper interpretation is requisite to understanding the general occupancy of this part of the site.

The floor level of Feature B is *ca.* 1 ft. lower than that of Feature A. At first, it appeared that Feature B was later than, and had been cut through, Feature A. Closer examination indicates that this is not the case. The only floor features associated with Feature B are two postholes and an undercut peripheral area, possibly used for storage. A hearth was found within the limits of the floor of Feature B, but there was almost 1 ft. of fill between the bottom of the hearth and the actual floor of Feature B; i.e., the hearth was at the same level as the floor of the immediately adjacent Feature A. This suggests that Feature B is the earlier of the two structures and that at some time it had been refloored with 1 ft. of earth and expanded to include what is here designated Feature A. The hearth in question was used in this remodelled and enlarged structure. Hence, the two construction periods indicated by Features B and A were probably separated by a relatively short time and represent a single occupation or component. If this interpretation is correct, the entrance, postholes, and hearth described for Feature A are also an integral part of Feature B, and the two features comprise a single pit house.

An adobe wall, oriented northwest-southeast, is superimposed above the edge of Features A and B. The associated floor (floor 1), 1 ft. below present ground surface, extends over the southwest half of Feature A. There was some indication that a storage pit had been dug from floor 1 into the pit-house fill, but the pit outlines could not be traced.

Slab-based walls transect the adobe wall (Table 5). Slight differences in elevation exist, the footing of the slab-based walls extending to the same level as floor 1 but not as deep as the footing of the adobe wall.

The two varieties of wall construction, the differences in depth of footing, and the alignment of fragmentary wall sections beyond this immediate area (cf. Table 5) all suggest two temporally distinct room-blocks with slightly different orientations. The simple adobe walls and associated floors represent the earlier room-block, the slab-based walls and associated features pertain to the latter.

Very few sherds were recovered from excavations in the vicinity of the pit house and the room-block(s). The small sample (Trenches 2, 2E) is apparently mixed and offers no evidence of stratigraphic differentiation. The major ceramic groups, Santa Fe B/W, unidentified B/W, Red Mesa B/W, neck-banded, and smooth-surfaced sherds, are all represented. The unidentified B/W and unpainted non-culinary sherds are all of the coarser paste with medium amounts of sherd temper and are of nonlocal origin presumably. Two neck-banded vessels (Pl. VIII *c, d*) were associated with the floor of the adobe-walled room above the pit house. The larger vessel had been sunk into a shallow pit and its orifice was at floor level. The smaller vessel rested on the floor.

The ceramic material, then, indicates a mixture of Santa Fe B/W and smeared-indented sherds with nonlocal painted pottery and neck-banded culinary vessels. The latter ceramic complex is similar to the material from the lower level of the kiva. The location of the two neck-banded vessels provides the single demonstrable association of a pottery type with an architectural feature in the immediate area. Evidently nonlocal painted pottery and neck-banded culinary vessels are associated with the adobe-walled room as in the kiva. It is reasonable to assume that the Santa Fe B/W and smeared-indented sherds are associated with the slab-based room-block, although this association cannot be demonstrated.

Sherds were found throughout the disturbed fill in the pit house, beneath the level of the poorly preserved floor of the adobe-walled room. At least one sherd of Red Mesa B/W was found immediately above the floor of Feature A. If any ceramic complex is associated with the pit house, it is apparently similar to that associated with the obviously later adobe-walled room. It is possible, but does not seem probable, that the pit house represents a non-ceramic occupation.

Exploratory trenches in other parts of Area B revealed fragmentary floor or occupation levels with tendencies to occur at depths of either 1 ft. 6 in. to 2 ft. or 2 ft. 6 in. to 3 ft. There were several cases of superposition. Much evidence of disturbance was observed in the fill and the ceramic assemblage showed considerable mixture. In those few cases for which ceramic associations could be ascertained, Santa Fe B/W and smeared-indented culinary sherds occurred in the upper levels (e.g. "floor 1" in trench 4), nonlocal painted wares, including Red Mesa B/W, and neck-banded culinary vessels occurred with the lower levels (e.g. "floor 2" in trench 4).

Two circular features (C and D) were found between the room-block area and the kiva. Neither had any floor features and their function is not known. They were called "adobe puddling pits," "borrow pits," and "storage areas" during the excavations; all of these interpretations appear equally reasonable. The association of Feature D with the early ceramic complex and the association of the occupation level ("floor 1") observed in the fill of this feature with Santa Fe B/W sherds is fairly secure. Feature C, located nearby, is more problematic, but its bottom was found at approximately the same depth as the occupation level in Feature D. It is most reasonable to assume that Feature C is associated with the late ceramic complex, although its fill contained a mixed ceramic sample.

INTERMEDIATE AREA

In the Intermediate Area, only Feature I provides evidence of a definite structure. (The excavations designated Feature II disclosed a shallowly buried floor or occupation level, but further interpretation is not warranted.)

Feature I is apparently a pit house. Its outline is quite irregular but roughly elliptical. A hearth area is located near the center of the structure and a large, undercut storage area was found on the northeast edge of the house. No well-defined posthole pattern was found; large posts tend to occur in the central part of the floor and smaller ones are located near the periphery.

A very small ceramic sample was obtained. A neck-banded sherd from the floor and the neck-banded and corrugated sherds from the fill suggest a pre-Kwahe'e Component occupation.

A sherd which had a squared rim bearing a single dot (or "tick") of carbon paint was found near floor level. Although this specimen cannot be identified as to type, it is of a class which is foreign to the Rio Grande Valley and characteristic of a relatively late period. Culinary pottery from both the fill and floor of Feature I suggests that the painted sherd is not associated with the occupation of the structure. If this interpretation is not correct, however, the pre-Kwahe'e status of the pit house would be quite doubtful.

The pit house in the Intermediate Area (Feature I) had many characteristics in common with the one in Area B. A pre-Kwahe'e ceramic complex is apparently associated with Feature I, but this occupation cannot be assigned specifically to either the Red Mesa complex or the pit-house occupation in Area B. Because of the absence of specific data and the paucity of associations in general, this occupation in the Intermediate Area will not be assigned to any specific cultural complex. It will be referred to as "Pit-house Occupation, Intermediate Area."

SUMMARY: OUTLINE OF CULTURAL COMPONENTS

The foregoing interpretation of the architectural and ceramic associations at the Tesuque By-Pass Site is summarized in Figure 9. Assuming the validity of this analysis, certain non-ceramic artifacts can be added to these associations and definitions of the individual occupations formulated. These are presented below, from late to early.

Santa Fe Component (found in Area B)

Architecture: Room-block with adobe floors and slab-based walls; outside storage pit; circular to elliptical floor areas of unknown use. No ceremonial structure located.

Pottery: Santa Fe B/W and smeared-indented culinary vessels.

Non-pottery artifacts: Worked sherds; small corner-notched projectile points; flake scrapers; flakes retouched about a point; turquoise; oval mano with one flat grinding surface; a thin stone (ventilator?) slab; split but unworked deer metapodial; large bird bone, probably eagle or turkey.

Remarks: Obsidian not a common raw material. The association of architectural remains and nonceramic artifacts with this occupation is not clear-cut, and this summary must be regarded as quite tentative.

Chronology: No dates were obtained on material from this component. Santa Fe B/W is a local Pueblo III pottery dated from *ca.* 1200 to 1350 A.D. (Stubbs and Stallings, 1953: Figure 70). The smeared-indented culinary pottery suggests that the Santa Fe Com-

LATE

SANTA FE COMPLEX

Santa Fe B/W, smeared-indented culinary vessels. Room-block with slab-based walls. Outside storage pit. Circular floor areas of unknown use, no floor features. All in Area B.

KWAHE'E COMPLEX

Kwahe'e B/W, corrugated and neck-banded culinary vessels. Room-block with slab-based walls. Circular, semi-subterranean kiva early; D-shaped kiva in room-block late. Rear rooms probably used for storage, front rooms as living quarters. Outside storage pits. Area A.

	RED MESA COMPLEX Unidentified mineral painted B/W, Red Mesa B/W, neck-banded culinary vessels. Painted pottery primarily nonlocal; some local painted wares in latest deposits. Adobe-walled room-block; semi-subterranean, circular kiva; circular to elliptical floor areas of unknown use, no floor features. All in Area B.
PIT-HOUSE OCCUPATION, INTERMEDIATE AREA Feature I EARLY	PIT-HOUSE OCCUPATION, AREA B Pit-house represented by Features A and B; probably some part of the Red Mesa ceramic complex. Area B.

Figure 9 – Architectural and ceramic complexes at the Tesuque By-Pass Site.

ponent at Tesuque By-Pass Site is not a particularly early Santa Fe B/W occupation, but the absence of later intrusive pottery and of side-notched points suggests a pre-1300 A.D. date.

Kwahe'e Component (found in Area A)

Architecture: L-shaped room-block with two banks of rooms. Both adobe and cobble floors; slab-based walls. Semi-subterranean circular kiva with rough masonry wall within angle of room-block, ventilator to southeast. Centrally located D-shaped chamber in room-block with possible ventilator opening to east, probably used for ceremonial purposes. Both inside and outside storage pits.

Pottery: Kwahe'e B/W, both neck-banded and shallowly corrugated culinary vessels.

Non-pottery artifacts: Worked sherds; curved and straight ceramic cloud-blowers; small corner-notched projectile points with expanding stems; flake scrapers; flakes retouched about a sharp point; other forms of chipped stone artifacts; trough metates open at one and two? ends; basin metates; rectangular manos with rounded corners and one flat grinding surface; wedge-sectioned manos with one and two flat grinding surfaces; chipped and ground axe with side and butt notches; grooved mauls; turquoise bead; bone awls (Types A, B, C); bird bone whistle; split and smoothed deer metapodial; one large bird bone; worked shell.

Remarks: lambdoidal or occipital deformation was noted on the two skulls associated with this component. Obsidian was a popular raw material in the rather limited chipped stone industry. Almost all remains from Area A belong to this component, and the Kwahe'e occupation is restricted to this portion of the site.

Chronology: No dates were obtained on material from this component. Kwahe'e B/W is a local Pueblo II pottery dated from *ca.* 1100 to 1200 A.D. (Stubbs and Stallings, 1953: Figure 70). The culinary vessels with shallow corrugations suggest that the Kwahe'e Component at the Tesuque By-Pass Site is relatively late in the Kwahe'e B/W period.

Red Mesa Component (found in Area B)

Architecture: Room-block with adobe walls and floors; circular to elliptical floor areas of unknown use; semi-subterranean circular kiva with walls of plastered native earth and ventilator to southeast.

Pottery: Unidentified B/W sherds decorated with mineral paint (including some Taos B/W?), Red Mesa B/W; neck-banded culinary vessels.

Non-pottery artifacts: Worked sherds, ceramic cloud-blower, small corner-notched projectile points with expanding stems, large corner-notched points or knives, flake scrapers; flakes retouched about a sharp point; other forms of stone artifacts; trough metates open at one end; oval and rectangular manos with one and two flat grinding surfaces; rectangular mano with rounded corners and finger groove; Type B and C bone awls, birdbone bead.

Remarks: Obsidian was not a common raw material. All pre-Kwahe'e structures in Area B except the pit house (Features A, B) have been placed in this component.

Chronology: No dates were obtained on material from this component. Absence of shallowly corrugated sherds on the one hand and of definite P I trade sherds on the other suggest a date of *ca.* 950 to 1100 A.D.

Pit-House Occupation, Area B

Architecture: Pit house designated Features A and B.

Pottery: Although no sherds can be definitely associated with this structure, it seems likely that a portion of the Red Mesa Component ceramic complex, including Red Mesa B/W, belongs with this structure.

Non-pottery artifacts: Oval manos, fragment of troughed metate. Possibly a few flake scrapers and a Type B bone awl.

Remarks: Definitely older than adobe-walled room-block ascribed to Red Mesa Component.

Chronology: Probably during the period 900 to 1100 A.D. This is a "guess date" based on presumed ceramic associations.

Pit-House Occupation, Intermediate Area

Architecture: Pit house designated Feature I.

Pottery: Neck-banded culinary ware. (Association of unidentified carbon-painted B/W sherd, found near floor, is doubtful.)

Non-pottery artifacts: Small projectile point, probably corner-notched with expanding stem; rectangular mano with rounded corners and one flat grinding surface; flake scrapers; snubnosed end scraper; hammerstone.

Remarks: Very little cultural material can be associated definitely with this structure. Architecture and the snub-nosed end scraper suggest that this may be a distinct (separate) occupation.

Chronology: Possibly during the period 900 to 1100 A.D. This is a "guess date" based on the absence of P I sherds on the one hand and upon the associated culinary sherds on the other.

II

COMPARISONS AND INTERPRETATIONS

INTRODUCTION

ANALYSIS of the cultural material from Tesuque By-Pass Site has led to the postulation of a series of communities, located at a specific place in the upper Rio Grande Valley. This sequence conforms to existing interpretations of early Puebloan occupations in the upper Rio Grande Valley (cf. Mera, 1935; Stubbs, *in* Stubbs and Stallings, 1953; Wendorf, 1954). None of the communities are entirely unique, and comparisons with other sites in adjacent areas will allow us to view each occupation as a part of the prehistoric settlement of the region.

The first section of the analysis is written, insofar as is possible, with reference only to the northern Rio Grande Valley proper. Comparisons and distributional data are restricted to the valley and, therefore, are not to be taken as exhaustive or complete for the whole Southwest, or even for the entire Rio Grande drainage basin. The immediate purpose is to present a picture of early Puebloan settlement in the northern Rio Grande area, and nothing more. It is all too easy to gloss over local developments and complexities by describing them as "reflections" or "resultants" of cultural traditions in other areas. I shall first attempt to relate the occupations of the Tesuque By-Pass Site to other developments in the immediate area. Relationships to other regions are discussed subsequently.

The mechanics of the comparative technique used herein are as follow:

1) The general distribution of the ceramic complex associated with each occupation at the Tesuque By-Pass Site is given. Such comments as are necessary regarding ceramic classification will be made at this point.

2) Excavated sites in the northern Rio Grande Valley which have comparable ceramic and architectural complexes are described briefly. An attempt is made to present data which seems pertinent to the Tesuque By-Pass material, but no attempt is made

to provide complete site summaries. The sites are presented in a general south to north order.

3) Inferences are made concerning the relation of the occupations at the Tesuque By-Pass Site to those at other sites, and the characteristics of the general culture type(s) are presented.

COMPARABLE OCCUPATIONS WITHIN THE RIO GRANDE VALLEY

RED MESA COMPONENT AND PIT-HOUSE OCCUPATION – AREA B.

Because the ceramic complexes of the Red Mesa Component and the pithouse occupation cannot be distinguished, they will be considered as a unit for purposes of comparisons. The pottery involved consists of Red Mesa B/W, unidentified black-on-white with exterior slip and mineral paint (including Taos B/W?), and neck-banded utility vessels.

Pottery similar to that which I have called Red Mesa B/W is found at many sites distributed throughout the trench of the northern Rio Grande Valley, from Red River south beyond Belen, N.M. (Fig. 10). This pottery is characterized by a heavy Kana-a style of decoration executed in mineral paint, a good white slip on bowl interiors and exteriors and on jar exteriors, and, usually, crushed sherd temper.

The name "Red Mesa B/W" was introduced by the Gladwins (1934), and was considered to be synonymous with Chaco I and Chaco Transitional Black-on-White by Hawley (*in* Kluckhohn and Reiter, 1939: 52). Hawley's bowls of this pottery type have no exterior slip. Similar pottery is discussed by Mera (1935: 3, 5, Pl. II) as "Chaco 2." Subsequently, the name Red Mesa B/W was extended to include well-slipped sherds such as those described in this report. Insofar as I can determine, the extension of "Red Mesa B/W" to Chaco 2 pottery has been virtually undocumented. At present, the name designates a horizon style found widely throughout the southwestern United States, in both Pueblo I and Pueblo II contexts, rather than a local pottery type. There is an obvious need to determine areal varieties of this type if its diagnostic value is to be increased. This task is complicated by many inescapable similarities of paste and temper associated with this pottery wherever it is found. The rather ubiquitous nature of Red Mesa B/W, as currently used, is probably responsible for the following statement by Stanley Stubbs: "Pueblo I and II Black-on-White pottery is the common denominator all across this region [the northern Rio Grande]. I do not think it proper

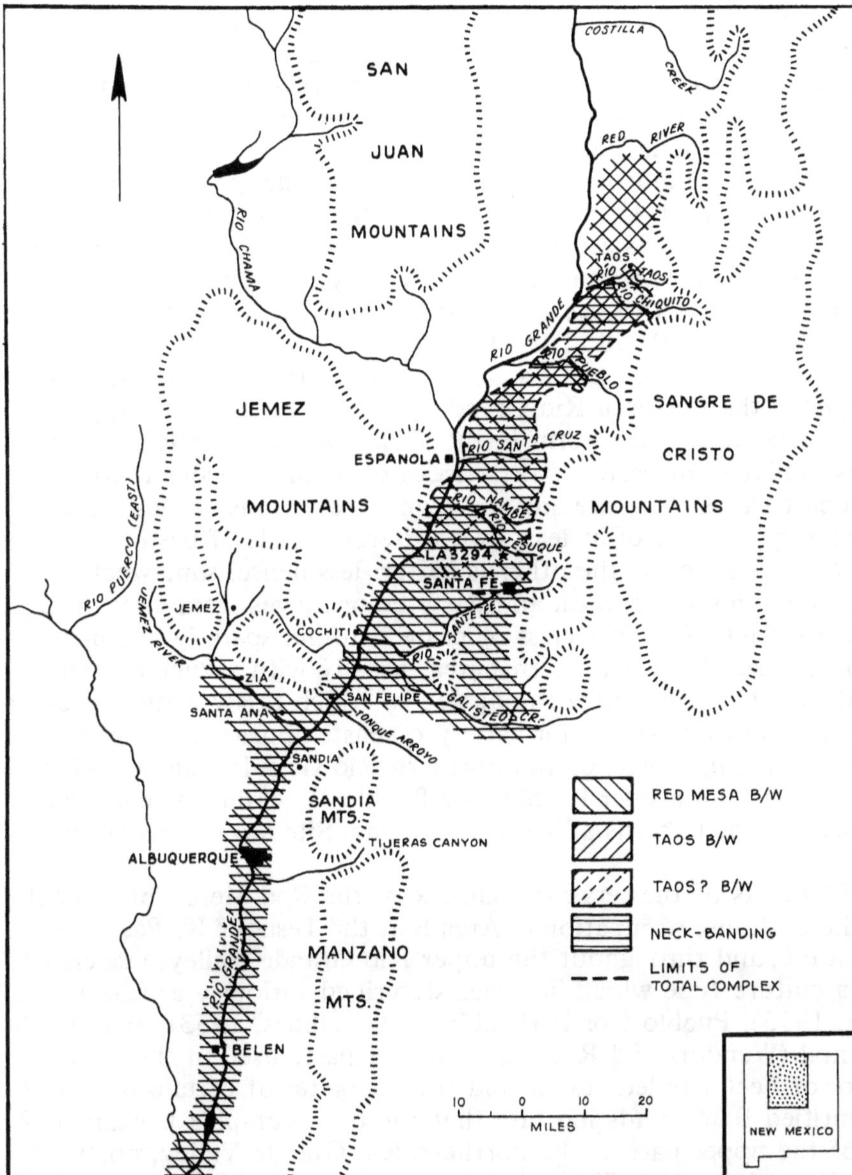

Figure 10 – Distribution in the Rio Grande Valley of Red Mesa Complex pottery types. Adapted from Mera, 1935.

to give a more exact name to the type at this time; Pueblo I or II, or Chaco I or II, to me, gives a time, space, and trait assemblage connotation which is lacking when a more localized name, such as Red Mesa Black-on-White is used" (Stubbs and Stallings, 1953: 154).

Sherds similar to much of the "unidentified B/W" from the Tesuque By-Pass Site are concentrated in the upper part of the northern Rio Grande Valley, in the vicinity of Taos between Red River and Rio Chiquito. This pottery has been designated Taos B/W (Mera, 1935:5-6, Pl. IV; see Map No. 1 for distribution), and is considered by Mera as a regional derivative of the Chaco 2 tradition. It must be noted, however, that the culinary pottery of the Taos area differs in many respects from that found at Tesuque By-Pass (cf. Blumenschein, 1958: 108-9).

Neck-banded culinary vessels are characteristic of sites scattered throughout the northern Rio Grande Valley, although they appear to be a relatively minor form in the Taos area. Very little information is available on paste characteristics or details of construction, but such data as there are and my own observations indicate that this pottery is made of at least two different kinds of paste: one is hard, dense, and gray, the other is softer, less dense, somewhat friable, contains some mica, and paste color ranges from gray through brown to black. The first class of paste is found sparsely at small sites in the southern part of this area, usually with a Pueblo I ceramic assemblage. I do not know the degree to which this variety is present north of Santa Fe. The latter variety of paste appears to be concentrated in the upper part of the northern Rio Grande Valley, and is often found with a later Pueblo I or Pueblo II ceramic assemblage. The neck-banded sherds at Tesuque By-Pass Site are of this latter variety.

Elements of the ceramic complex of the Red Mesa Component and the pit-house occupation in Area B at the Tesuque By-Pass Site, then, are found throughout the upper Rio Grande Valley, associated with a culture type which has been described variously as Chaco 2 (Mera, 1935), Pueblo I or II (Stubbs and Stallings, 1953), and Developmental (Wendorf and Reed, 1955). The paste used in the manufacture of neck-banded vessels and the character of certain of the unidentified B/W sherds indicate that the total complex is characteristic of the upper part of the northern Rio Grande Valley, north of Santa Fe and south of Taos.

Excavated sites in the northern Rio Grande Valley which have more or less comparable ceramic assemblages are few and far between.

Such information as has come to my attention is summarized in the following paragraphs.

In the southern part of the area under consideration, there are seven small sites at which are found circular structures closely comparable to the kiva of the Red Mesa Component in Area B. These features are interpreted variously as kivas and pithouses. One site (L.A. 586) is in Tijeras Canyon, about 20 miles east of Albuquerque (Wendorf, n.d.), three sites are near Sandia Pueblo (Peckham, 1957), one is near Zia Pueblo (Vytlacil and Brodie, 1958), one is near Santa Ana Pueblo (Allen and McNutt, 1955), and one is in the vicinity of San Felipe Pueblo (Peckham, 1954). These sites, discussed at greater length in a following section, must be considered briefly here, in order to place them in proper perspective with the Red Mesa material from Tesuque By-Pass.

Small and architecturally simple surface structures are present at four of these sites, but none are comparable to the well-constructed adobe-walled room of the Red Mesa period at Tesuque By-Pass.

There are no structures at any of these sites which are similar to the pit house in Area B. At one of the sites near Sandia Pueblo, there is a semi-subterranean structure, oval in outline, with undercut storage pits and an irregular roof support pattern. It has a central fireplace and no entry or ventilator projection was found (Peckham, 1957: 47-48, Fig. 20). At the site near San Felipe, irregularly shaped structures interpreted as surface jacales have amorphous roof-post patterns and no central hearths, but lack undercut storage pits and entry or ventilator projections (Peckham, 1954: 43-46, Fig. 4, upper).

Red Mesa B/W is the dominant painted pottery at most, but not all, of these sites. It is almost invariably associated with early Basketmaker III-Pueblo I intrusives such as Kiatuthlanna B/W, Whitemound B/W, Lino B/G, San Marcial B/W, Alma Plain, and Mogollon R/Br. Culinary vessels are either plain (usually classified as Lino Gray, characteristic of Basketmaker III) or neck-banded (classified as Kana-a Gray, a Pueblo I derivative of Lino), but neck-banded sherds occur in lower proportions than were found at Tesuque By-Pass. This latter fact, plus the early intrusive sherds, suggests that these seven sites represent initial occupations which are earlier than the Red Mesa period(s) at Tesuque By-Pass.

These seven sites provide my only documentary information concerning excavated ceramic occupations within the Rio Grande Valley between Isleta Pueblo in the south and the Tesuque By-Pass Site which are as early as, or earlier than, the Red Mesa Component. Although none of the sites closely resembles the occupation at Tesuque

By-Pass, they do indicate that many elements of the latter were present within the northern Rio Grande Valley at an earlier time period. The elements concerned are discussed in detail in a following section.

Excavations by Stanley Stubbs at Site L.A. 835, approximately seven miles north (downstream) from the Tesuque By-Pass Site and on the opposite side of Rio Tesuque, exposed what will be the most important early Pueblo site in the northern Rio Grande Valley.

Two brief notes have been published regarding these excavations (Stubbs and Stallings, 1953: 155; Stubbs, 1954). The site consists of 12 to 15 house units, each containing some 10 to 20 rooms. Several types of wall construction are present, but slab-based adobe construction is apparently predominant. One or more kivas are associated with each room-block, and a great variety of kivas was found. A "great kiva," some 52 ft. in diameter, has crude masonry walls, and eight roof supports. Circular and rectangular kivas, both above ground and subterranean, are present. Stubbs dates this site, on the basis of the associated pottery, as primarily of the eleventh century, with a terminal date of approximately 1150 A.D. (Stubbs, 1954: 45).

Although the pottery analysis is not yet complete, Stubbs has very kindly given me full access to such notes as he has made. His ceramic classification does not employ the usual "Red Mesa B/W," "Taos B/W," "Kwahe'e B/W" terminology, but is based rather on specific attributes, such as slip and temper (cf. Stubbs, 1954: 45). For this reason, any parallels which I impute to named types from the Tesuque By-Pass Site are my responsibility and do not necessarily reflect Stubbs' analysis.

The major ceramic categories at L.A. 835 are, I think, almost the same as those at the Tesuque By-Pass Site: Red Mesa B/W; presumably sherds similar to the unidentified B/W; Kwahe'e B/W; neck-banded, corrugated, and plain culinary vessels. There is a tendency for neck-banded sherds to be associated with painted pottery comparable to Red Mesa and the unidentified B/W sherds, and for corrugated pottery to be associated with sherds comparable to Kwahe'e B/W. There is, however, no clear division between the two complexes.

In some structures of the site, including the "great kiva," there seems to be, if not a pre-Kwahe'e occupation, at least a preponderance of ceramic material comparable to the Red Mesa sherds from Tesuque By-Pass. My impression is that the major portion of the occupation at L.A. 835 is slightly later than the Red Mesa period at Tesuque By-Pass. The complex and diverse nature of the architectural features at the former site will have a great effect upon our interpretations of both the Red Mesa and Kwahe'e periods in the northern Rio Grande Valley.

A number of subterranean structures are reported from the vicinity of Taos, New Mexico, in the Hondo Valley, above Taos Creek Valley, and near Pot Creek (Blumenschein, 1956, 1958). Excavations have been conducted in the Hondo Valley only. Associated pottery includes "black-on-white trade wares of general Chacoan ancestry" and of a time period of about A.D. 1000 to 1150, possibly a small amount of locally made Taos B/W, and early forms of Taos Incised, together with large amounts of culinary ware (Blumenschein, 1956: 55). The great majority of the culinary pottery is smooth-surfaced plain gray ware, many sherds of which undoubtedly come from the lower portions of vessels with variously modified rims. Major classes of textured rim and neck sherds are "plain incised," "accentuated coil," "smoothed coil" and "deeply incised," in order of decreasing popularity (Blumenschein 1958: 108-9). Neither neck-banding nor corrugated sherds appear to be common, although the relationship of "accentuated" and "smoothed" coils to neck-bands is not clear.

Here, then, we have painted pottery which is roughly similar to that of the pre-Kwahe'e period, but associated with culinary vessels which show an emphasis on incised decoration.

Five deep subterranean structures were excavated or tested. Four are square or rectangular and one is approximately circular; all are interpreted as pit houses. All structures had central fireplaces with raised adobe rims, walls plastered over native earth, probably ventilators on their east side, and lacked sipapus. In two cases excavation was sufficient to determine the roof support pattern. A four-post support pattern was found in one of the square structures, and two posts were located near opposite ends of a diameter of the circular structure.

Associated artifacts include slab and trough metates, full-grooved mauls, chipped pebble axes (Blumenschein, 1958: 109) and a single stone elbow pipe (Lambert, 1956). Obsidian was evidently not a favored raw material.

The sites discussed above, from near Sandia Pueblo in the south to just beyond Taos Pueblo in the north, have ceramic complexes which are probably as early as, or earlier than, the Red Mesa period represented in Area B at the Tesuque By-Pass Site. I know of no other useable descriptions of equally early sites in the area of immediate concern. As will be seen later, there are roughly comparable sites in adjacent areas and there are sites within the Rio Grande Valley which appear to be only slightly later than the Red Mesa period. At present, however, we are in a position to summarize the information available on the Red Mesa occupations of the northern Rio Grande Valley.

The discriminating reader will have noticed that, of the sites discussed, none is entirely similar to the Red Mesa Component at Tesuque By-Pass. The distribution of Red Mesa B/W and neck-banded culinary vessels is almost pan-northern Rio Grande Valley. The data from the Taos area suggest that neck-banded sherds may have never achieved popularity in the uppermost portion of the area. Pottery comparable to many of the unidentified B/W sherds from Tesuque By-Pass is not widely distributed, but restricted to this same northern (Taos) area (see distribution of Taos B/W, Fig. 10; Mera, 1935: Map No. 1; Stubbs and Stallings, 1953: Fig. 69). Neither Taos B/W nor sherds similar to this type seem to be found in any number to the south of Santa Fe.

Sites in the southern part of our area at which Red Mesa B/W and neck-banded culinary vessels are present also have early intrusives from Basketmaker III and early Pueblo I ceramic complexes. At several of these sites there are early brown ware sherds, such as Alma Plain, Mogollon R/Br, and other unidentified red-on-brown sherds, presumably from the Mogollon area to the south. These early intrusives, black-on-white and red-on-brown, do not seem to be characteristic of the sites north of White Rock Canyon (above Cochiti Pueblo) and La Bajada Hill (north of the lower Santa Fe River). There is no known BM III or Pueblo I pottery indigenous to the Rio Grande Valley north of the White Rock-La Bajada axis. The implication is that Puebloan sites of the BM III and formative P I stages are virtually absent from the uppermost Rio Grande Valley.

This inference is most important to the interpretation of pre-Kwahe'e (e.g. Red Mesa) occupations in the area of concern, and it is pertinent to comment upon extant hypotheses concerning the earliest ceramic occupations in the northern Rio Grande Valley.

H. P. Mera (1935), in his classic work on the Rio Grande Valley, states that in the area north of the 35th degree of latitude (which crosses the Rio Grande ca. 6 miles south of Albuquerque)

> sites showing nothing but true Basket Maker pottery are quite rare . . . and it seems probable that a great deal of the Basket Maker III pottery of this eastern region is more representative of the final phase of that cultural stage and may well be considered as transitional between typical Basket Maker III and the immediately following ceramic development, Chaco 1. To date, only one site of this class (L.A. 177), situated in the valley of the Rio Santa Fe, has failed to show at least one decorated sherd. Basket Maker locations in this region are known only in the form of sherd areas. . . .

With regard to Chaco I, or Pueblo I, sites, he continues:

> Pure sites containing Chaco I pottery . . . though more numerous than those of the B.M. 3 period, are comparatively few in number but are found to extend over a range somewhat greater than that covered by the latter [p. 3].

Trade wares described are black-on-red (presumably La Plata), red- or black-on-orange (presumably Abajo), and southern brownware. The black-on-red pottery is found sparingly and the (presumably) Abajo intrusives occur at only one site (L.A. 195) within the Rio Grande Valley proper. L.A. 195 is in Rio Arriba County, well to the north of Tesuque By-Pass. Inspection of the site collection indicates the presence of Red Mesa B/W at this site.

In plotting the distribution of Basketmaker III and Chaco I sites in the Rio Grande Valley proper, Mera does not distinguish between pottery of the two stages. Sherd areas of one or both periods were found primarily south of the mouth of the Santa Fe River, and sporadically in the area between the Tesuque Valley and a point just north of Espanola (L.A. 195). A single site is located on the Rio Grande west and slightly north of Santa Fe.

Stubbs discusses the early occupation of the upper Rio Grande in terms of "the period ca. A.D. 700-1000 – Chaco I and II, Pueblo I and II, or Developmental Pueblo" and, concerning earlier occupations, says only "On the basis of present evidence, the Basketmaker III phase is very rare or missing in most sections of the upper Rio Grande area" (Stubbs and Stallings, 1953: 152-53).

Wendorf and Reed, in their reconstruction of northern Rio Grande prehistory, set the southern limit of the area somewhat more to the south than does Stubbs. In discussing "The Rio Grande Developmental Period (*ca.* A.D. 600-1200)" they state that "Ceramic sites which could be correlated with San Juan Anasazi, Basketmaker III or early Pueblo I are extremely rare in the northern Rio Grande (Wendorf and Reed, 1955:138). They mention two sites near Albuquerque and describe L.A. 177 as "possibly of this age" (p. 138). They continue,

> Sites contemporary with Pueblo I are also small but more numerous than those of the preceding phase. The area of known occupation extended as far north as the mouth of the Chama . . . These contain, in addition to the pottery types of the Basketmaker III sites, neck-banded gray and brown wares (Kana-a Gray, Alma Neck-Banded), Kiatuthlanna Black-on-white, and, occasionally, La Plata Black-on-red and Abajo Black-on-orange [p. 138].

Two sites are discussed: one near Santa Ana (Allen and McNutt, 1955) and one near San Felipe (Peckham, 1954). Both of these sites, mentioned previously, are south of the White Rock Canyon-La Bajada Hill area and provided the only excavation data available at the time. The distribution of early sites adds nothing to that given by Mera, and no new early ceramic sites are described for the uppermost part of the Rio Grande Valley.

Insofar as I know, none of the BM III-early P I sites north of the White Rock-La Bajada axis has been excavated as of this date (1959). Many, if not all, of them may represent the expansion of the Chaco I or Pueblo I groups, postulated by Mera. With but two possible exceptions (L.A. 171, 195), both very tentative, there is virtually no specific information which contradicts the hypothesis that Puebloan groups were not in the Rio Grande Valley north of White Rock Canyon and La Bajada Hill before 800 A.D. Furthermore, the very small number of sites which seem to be pre-Pueblo II suggests that Puebloan occupation of this northernmost area had begun but was still quite minimal in the period 800-900 A.D.

Now, to return to the Red Mesa period at Tesuque By-Pass. It is basically late Pueblo I-early Pueblo II, and represents some of the earliest excavated material in the northern section of the upper Rio Grande Valley. Its closest analogue, from an architectural and ceramic standpoint, was found in the earliest occupation of L.A. 835. Other ceramic ties exist with the early sites in the Taos area. Although the material from these sites differs in several respects from, and may be slightly later than, the Tesuque By-Pass material, the data all suggest one important conclusion. The Red Mesa (and possibly the earliest Kwahe'e) period is characterized by a well-developed Pueblo complex, ceramically mature and architecturally diversified.

With regard to ceramics, in addition to neck-banded culinary vessels, painted pots of several shapes and ornamented in at least two styles of decoration were used by the pre-Kwahe'e inhabitants of the immediate area. These vessels may or may not have been obtained by trade, but they were available.

In the Taos region, a different tradition of culinary vessels was present; some painted vessels were obtained by trade, and at least one style of painted pottery (found at Tesuque By-Pass and grouped with the unidentified B/W) seems to have been produced locally. It is of considerable interest that pottery which is quite probably an early variety of Taos B/W was available to the inhabitants of the Tesuque By-Pass Site somewhat earlier than was Kwahe'e B/W pottery. Pit-houses, adobe-walled room-blocks, and circular kivas were apparently constructed during this period at Tesuque By-Pass. When the data from L.A. 835 are available, it is quite probable that other forms of architecture will be added to this inventory. Still another distinctive architectural form, square and/or rectangular subterranean dwellings, is present in the Taos area during this period or soon thereafter.

Due to the virtual absence of occupations in the immediate area which may be taken as ancestral to these developments, it is most reasonable to consider the Red Mesa occupations as remains of immigrants from some Puebloan center outside the northern Rio Grande Valley proper. The Red Mesa Component at Tesuque By-Pass and the earliest occupation at L.A. 835 seem to be sufficiently similar to indicate a common source.

Food remains were not plentiful, but it is probable that these people were the first agriculturalists in the upper valley, for corn, beans, and squash were established crops in other Puebloan areas. It is likely that they also relied upon deer and antelope for meat (and clothing?), as did the people of the subsequent Kwahe'e Component. The period is probably no earlier than 900 A.D., and it is doubtful that any Puebloan groups were in the area prior to 800 A.D.

The comparable but distinctive remains in the Taos region indicate that the question of single or multiple origins for the early ceramic period in the area must not be answered hastily.

PIT-HOUSE OCCUPATION – INTERMEDIATE AREA

The pit-house in the Intermediate Area (Feature I) is interpreted as a pre-Kwahe'e, Pueblo II, occupation on the basis of a very few sherds which were associated with the structure. The architecture and the snub-nosed endscraper suggest that this occupation may be distinct from the pre-Kwahe'e occupations in Area B, but this inference is extremely tentative.

The survey of sites made in the preceding section offers little analogous material. One rather striking architectural parallel may be pointed out. At one of the sites near Sandia (L.A. 3290) there was found an oval structure with unplastered walls and floor, a large undercut peripheral storage pit, an irregular roof-post pattern, and a clay-lined central hearth. No indication of an entry was found. No painted sherds were identified in this structure, and the bulk of the pottery was classified as Lino Gray (16 sherds) and Kana-a Gray (1 sherd). Peckham notes that the single diagnostic sherd (Kana-a Gray, neck-banded) which comes from the fill indicates, tenuously, a Pueblo I occupation of the pithouse. The site itself has structures which are interpreted as BM III, P I, and P I or early P II (see Peckham, 1957: 47-48, 67ff., Fig. 27).

It is difficult to evaluate the significance of this comparison between such non-specific attributes as "roughly oval but irregular house outline," "irregular roof-post pattern," "unprepared floors and walls," "irregularly shaped peripheral storage pits," etc., but the parallels remain. These architectural similarities can be taken to indicate that the Intermediate Area occupation was earlier instead of later than the Red Mesa period in Area B. If this is so, Feature I is the earliest excavated structure at the Tesuque By-Pass Site, representing a very late Pueblo I or early Pueblo II occupation which may date as early as 850 A.D.

On the other hand, the single unidentified B/W sherd may indicate that the fill, and inferrentially the occupation, of this pithouse is later than that of the Red Mesa period in Area B. If this is the case, the pithouse is a Pueblo II period structure which probably dates 1000-1100 A.D.

The latter interpretation is perhaps the more reasonable, but I cannot feel strongly inclined toward either.

KWAHE'E COMPONENT – AREA A

The major elements of the ceramic complex of the Kwahe'e Component are Red Mesa B/W, Kwahe'e B/W, neck-banded and corrugated culinary vessels. Red Mesa B/W and neck-banded culinary vessels are present in relatively small proportions; their distribution, virtually pan-northern Rio Grande Valley, has been presented above.

Corrugated culinary vessels are widely distributed throughout the Southwest, within the northern Rio Grande Valley and elsewhere. I have no specific data on the degree to which corrugated vessels replaced the plain and incised culinary tradition in the Taos area, but they were present in the southern part of that region (Jeançon, 1929: 20).

Kwahe'e B/W is found in the Rio Grande Valley to the mouth of the Rio Chama in the north and south to a point just north of Albuquerque. On the east side of the river, however, it is not common south of Galisteo Creek. The greatest concentration of Kwahe'e B/W appears to be east of the Rio Grande, between the Galisteo and the mouth of the Chama (Fig. 11; see also Mera, 1935: Map No. 1; Stubbs and Stallings, 1953: 154). Kwahe'e B/W is considered to be a local development from the earlier Chaco I-II (Red Mesa B/W as the term is used here) pottery, beginning in the late eleventh century. The terminal date of this pottery type is *ca.* 1200 A.D. It should be noted that Taos B/W is considered to be another local derivation of the same Red Mesa B/W (Mera, 1935: 6; Stubbs, *in* Smiley, Stubbs, and Ban-

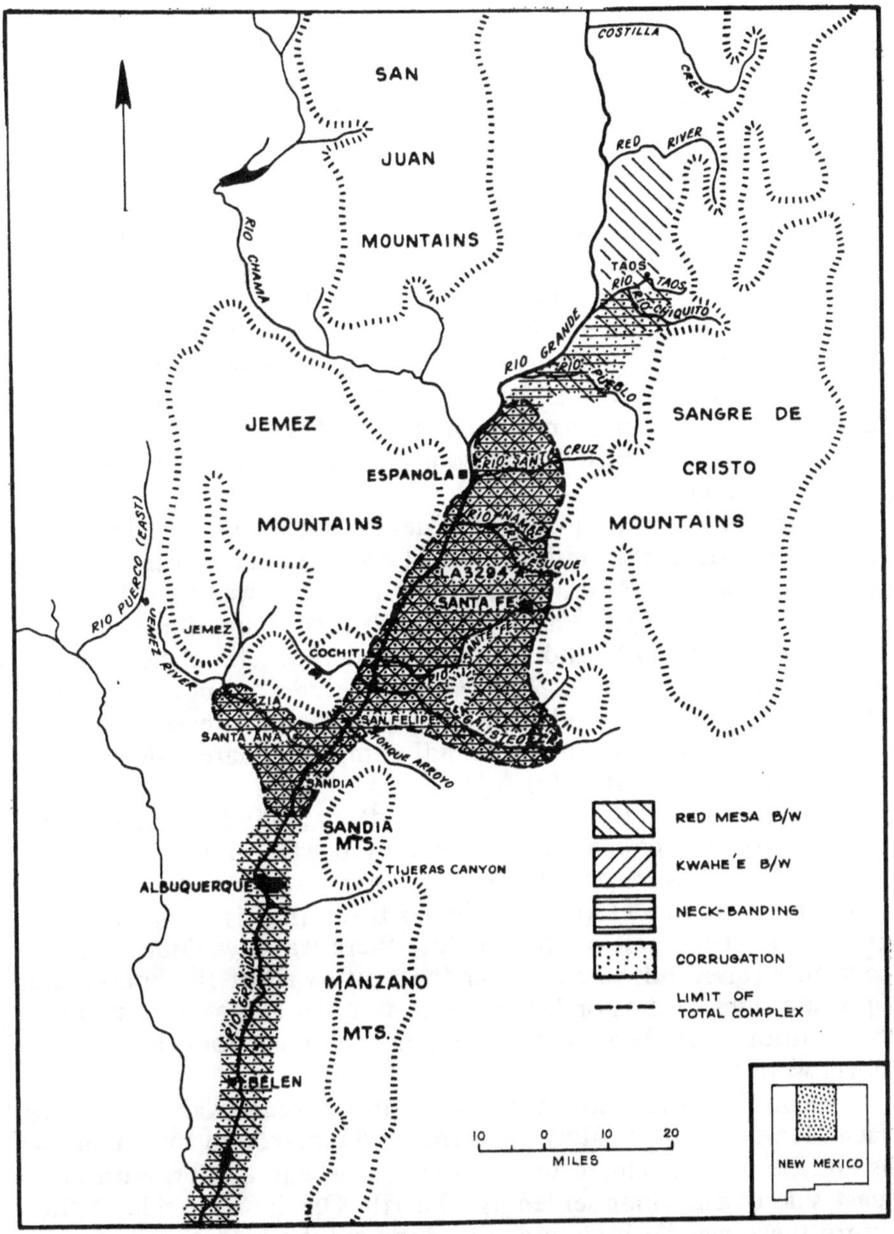

Figure 11 – Distribution in the Rio Grande Valley of Kwahe'e Complex pottery types. Adapted from Mera, 1935.

nister, 1953: 61). In the region north of the Chama and south of Taos, sherds are found which appear to be transitional between Kwahe'e B/W and Taos B/W (Peckham, personal communication).

Because Red Mesa B/W, neck-banded culinary vessels, and corrugated culinary vessels are so widely distributed, the distribution of the Kwahe'e Component's total ceramic complex, as a whole, can be equated to that of Kwahe'e B/W.

Before turning to such information as is available from site excavations, it seems appropriate to reiterate an observation which has been made by nearly all students concerned with the northern Rio Grande Valley: the appearance of Kwahe'e B/W is coincident with an expansion and increased intensity of Puebloan occupation in this area. The site files at the Laboratory of Anthropology in Santa Fe indicate that Kwahe'e B/W is to be found on approximately one hundred sites in the northern Rio Grande Valley and immediately adjacent areas. There must be, of course, many more which have not been recorded.

During the excavation of Pindi Pueblo (Stubbs and Stallings, 1953), approximately six miles south of Santa Fe and on the north bank of the Santa Fe River, an early ceramic level was partially exposed. The painted pottery associated with this occupation is described as Red Mesa B/W and closely related types, Kwahe'e B/W, Wingate B/Red and Puerco B/Red. Culinary wares are not described in detail, but only as "coiled; incised and striated; plain ware" (Stubbs and Stallings, 1953: 14). This pre-Pindi complex is dated, dendrochronologically, at about 1200 A.D.

Two structures were associated with the pre-Pindi horizon. One was a jacal, roughly equilateral with excurved walls and rounded corners. The walls were oriented roughly north-south and east-west and were nine to ten feet long. On the north-south axis of the structure and in the northern half of the building there was a well-made fireplace with a raised adobe rim. Near the south wall of the house, and on opposite sides of the north-south axis, two flat stones were set in adobe at floor level. The structure had no prepared floor, and no roof supports were found.

A second pre-Pindi structure, semi-subterranean, was located near the jacal. It was approximately eight feet in diameter and three feet deep. Walls and floors were unplastered native earth, and a depression in the east side of the floor served as a hearth. On the west side of the structure there was "a broken-down, sloping cut which may have served as an entrance way, or vestibule, but it was too damaged to determine its original shape" (Stubbs and Stallings, 1953: 25). A single, centrally-located roof post was found. Sherds from the lower fill of this structure are described as early Kwahe'e and Chaco II Black-on-white.

Very few artifacts were recovered from the pre-Pindi horizon, but a trough metate (open at one end) and a Type B bone awl are listed (Stubbs and Stallings, 1953: 116, 130).

The pre-Pindi ceramic complex is similar to that of the Kwahe'e Component at Tesuque By-Pass with regard to Red Mesa B/W, Kwahe'e B/W, neck-banded (coiled) and plain culinary vessels, and differs only in that no corrugated sherds were found in the small ceramic sample at the former site. Data from Pindi do not permit a comparison of the degree to which individual elements of the ceramic complex are present. Two new architectural forms are added to the Kwahe'e inventory: the jacal and a small pithouse. The latter structure has certain general characteristics in common with the pre-Kwahe'e pit houses at Tesuque By-Pass.

Site L.A. 835 (Stubbs and Stallings, 1953: 155; Stubbs, 1954) has been mentioned above, in the discussion of the Red Mesa material. Although some structures at this site may well belong to this earlier period, the greatest part of the occupation at L.A. 835 is Kwahe'e. This is the largest site of this period which has been excavated.

The painted pottery is apparently similar to Red Mesa B/W and Kwahe'e B/W at Tesuque By-Pass; culinary vessels were plain, neck-banded, and corrugated. Other minor forms, such as incised vessels, are present, just as they are at Tesuque By-Pass. In short, the ceramic complexes of L.A. 835 and of the Kwahe'e Component consist of the same elements, but again, data are not available which permit quantitative comparison.

The diversified architectural complex at L.A. 835 not only duplicates the room-block and circular kiva at Tesuque By-Pass, but adds new elements to the inventory: rectangular kivas, above and below ground; upright pole reinforcement in subterranean walls; Great Kiva (possibly earlier); several wall construction techniques using stone and adobe singly or in combination; a village pattern of several distinct room-blocks, each with its associated ceremonial structure(s). The room-blocks themselves are somewhat distinctive: a row of relatively large (12 to 16 ft.) square rooms with firepits, presumably living quarters, in front of smaller rectangular rooms, probably used for storage (Stubbs, 1954: 43).

Artifacts were not abundant at the site, but trough metates open at one and both ends, tri-notched axes with polishing confined mainly to the blade, and ornaments of turquoise, shell, and jet are mentioned (Stubbs, 1954: 44).

Three burials were excavated. One had an undeformed skull, one showed lambdoidal deformation, one vertical occipital deformation.

These two sites, Pindi and L.A. 835, provide the only Kwahe'e occupations described in any detail in the literature. A few additional sites have been excavated but not reported; specifically, Arroyo Negro (L.A. 114) on the Santa Fe River and about three miles west of Santa Fe, Mocho (L.A. 191) on Arroyo Hondo about six miles south of Santa Fe, Tesuque Valley Ruin (L.A. 742) about ten miles north of Santa Fe. There is probably a Kwahe'e and Red Mesa occupation beneath La Garrita, within the city limits of Santa Fe (B.T. Ellis, personal communication). A limited amount of information is available on some of these sites in Wendorf and Reed (1955: 140-42, Fig. 2, Fig. 3), and tree-ring dates for some of them have been published by Smiley, Stubbs and Bannister (1953). It may be noted that the latter are often difficult to evaluate, because many of the sites are multi-component. Wendorf and Reed (1955:142) note that the dates range from 963 to 1194 A.D., with the greatest concentration at 1050-1150 A.D. These same authors consider these sites as "essentially the same" (p. 140), and it can be assumed that the unpublished sites would not add any further major ceramic or architectural elements to our present list.

The Kwahe'e Component at Tesuque By-Pass, then, is typical of a well-developed and widespread Pueblo complex in the northern Rio Grande Valley. Chronological evidence indicates that the Kwahe'e occupations were characteristic between 1100 and 1200 A.D.; they quite probably appeared in the area by 1050 A.D. Surface surveys indicate that the period is one of expansion and population increase, with the greatest concentration of sites in the valley between the mouth of the Chama in the north and Galisteo Creek in the south. The few excavated sites are concentrated in the vicinity of Santa Fe and the nearby Tesuque Valley.

Very little perishable material has been recovered from sites of this period, but occasional charred corn cobs, the abundance of manos and trough metates, and large numbers of animal bones (see Appendix) indicate that both agriculture and hunting were basic to the subsistence of these people.

All evidence indicates a fairly continuous transition from earlier pre-Kwahe'e complexes (as found in Area B at Tesuque By-Pass) into the Kwahe'e period, although several new traits appear in the area.

There is great elaboration of architecture, both domestic and religious. Religious architecture includes circular kivas below ground (probably the commonest form), circular kivas above ground, rectangular kivas above and below ground, and Great Kivas. Construction features used in religious structures include pole-reinforced walls and crude masonry, four-post roof support, sipapus, central fireplaces with raised adobe rims, ash pits, ventilators to the south or southeast.

In ceramics, there is a change in design emphasis, mineral paint remains in vogue, and the quality of the slip deteriorates. Also during the Kwahe'e period, corrugated culinary vessels appear and finally surpass neck-banded vessels in popularity.

Artifacts characteristic of this period include tubular and elbow pipes of clay, trough metates open at one and both ends, small corner-notched obsidian points with expanding stems, mammal bone awls, tri- or poly-notched axes with polished bits, full-grooved mauls, bird bone whistles, ornaments of turquoise, jet, and shell. Many other artifact types are also present, but in minor proportions.

Head deformation was practiced to some degree during this period.

Intrusive sherds indicate relations with other areas of the Southwest, and shell ornaments show that the northern Rio Grande Valley was connected with at least some of the major trade routes of the western United States.

The marked population expansion and the appearance of new traits would suggest continued immigration into the area. The gradual transition from pre-Kwahe'e to Kwahe'e complexes, seen at several sites, further suggests that the Kwahe'e period immigrants were not radically different from their predecessors in the area. It seems likely, but virtually impossible to demonstrate, that local population growth in the Rio Grande Valley also added to the Puebloan expansion during the Kwahe'e period.

SANTA FE COMPONENT – AREA B

The ceramic complex associated with this occupation consists of Santa Fe B/W, smeared-indented culinary vessels, and possibly some plain-surfaced culinary vessels.

Santa Fe B/W is found in the northern Rio Grande Valley from the Rio Pueblo and Rio Chama area in the north to the Jemez River and Galisteo Basin in the south (Fig. 12; see also Mera, 1935: Map. No. 2; Stubbs and Stallings, 1953: 48, Fig. 69). This pottery, thought to have developed locally from Kwahe'e B/W *ca.* 1200-1350 A.D., is considered to indicate the beginning of Pueblo III (Stubbs and Stallings, 1953: 48, 154, Fig. 70) and/or the Rio Grande Coalition Period (Wendorf and Reed, 1955: 143-44).

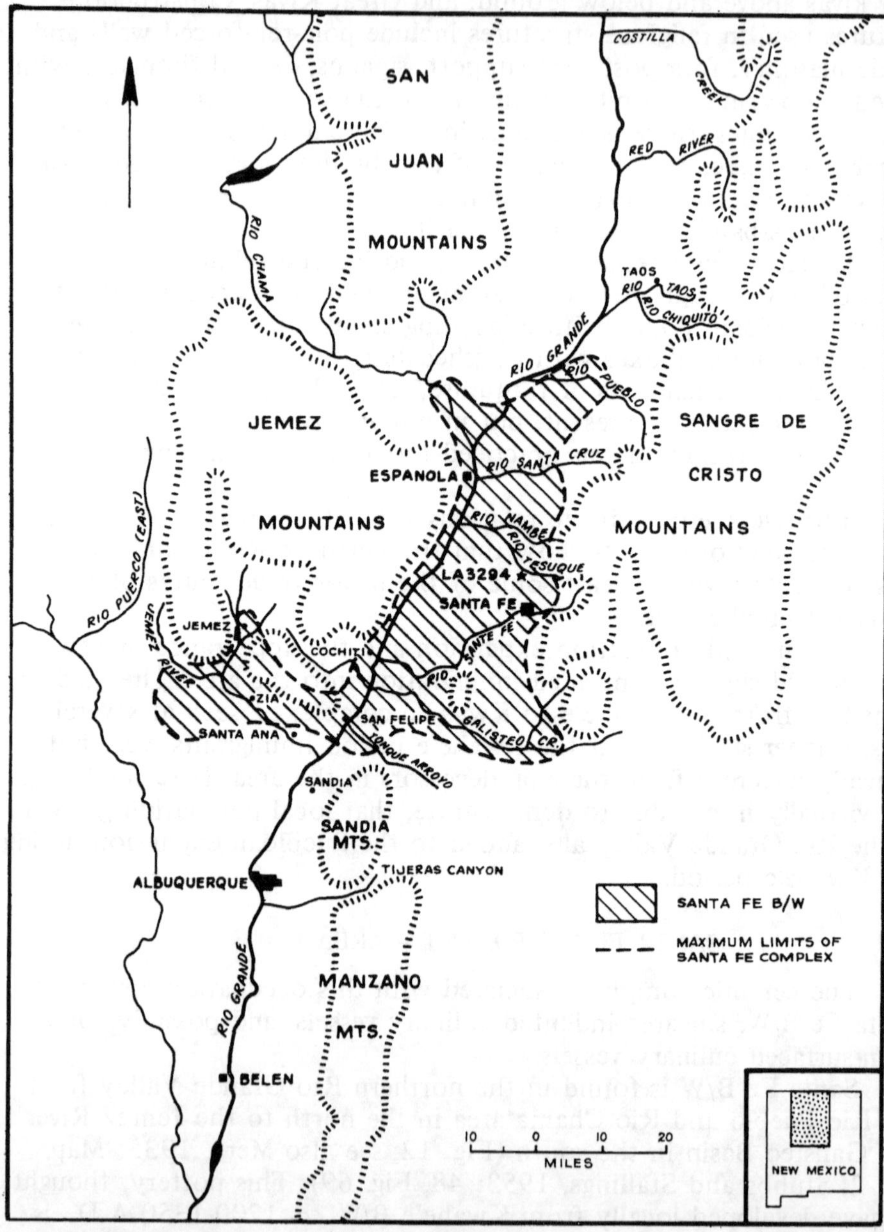

Figure 12 – Distribution in the Rio Grande Valley of Santa Fe B/W pottery. Adapted from Mera, 1935.

The distribution of smeared-indented vessels such as are found at Tesuque By-Pass is presumably the same as that of Santa Fe B/W (Mera, 1935: 14), but it is nowhere given in detail. These vessels represent one of the earliest of the highly characteristic Rio Grande culinary wares. A number of surface treatments have been recognized, but almost all share the quality of being smoothed subsequent to an initial surface manipulation. This secondary treatment, not unknown in other areas of the United States, inevitably produces classificatory problems. Perhaps this explains the virtual absence of detailed study of the Rio Grande culinary wares since the very excellent discussions by the late H. P. Mera.

The distribution of the ceramic complex associated with the Santa Fe Component at Tesuque By-Pass, then, may be taken as that of Santa Fe B/W pottery in the northern Rio Grande Valley.

If one can judge at all by the number of recorded sites, the Santa Fe period in the Rio Grande is one of further population increase. (The ratio of sites with Santa Fe B/W present to sites with Kwahe'e B/W present, as recorded in the site files of the Laboratory of Anthropology, Santa Fe, is almost 3 to 1; the period of manufacture of the two types is approximately equal.)

Information from excavated sites is greater than for the earlier periods, and a summary of available data can be found in Wendorf and Reed (1955: 143-48). Because there is virtually nothing but the ceramic complex of the Santa Fe Component at Tesuque By-Pass to use in comparisons with other sites, the following paragraphs will emphasize pottery. Almost all excavated sites that produce Santa Fe B/W have very elaborate ceramic assemblages, with later types of painted pottery well represented, if not predominant. These later pottery types were not present at the Tesuque By-Pass Site, and will not be discussed.

There is, in effect, no information concerning sites in which Santa Fe B/W is characteristic of a terminal occupation, as it is at Tesuque By-Pass. Such sites exist, and two may have been excavated. At Arroyo Negro (L.A. 114) and Mocho (L.A. 191), both mentioned above with regard to the Kwahe'e Component, indigenous pottery is described as Chaco II B/W, Red Mesa B/W, Kwahe'e B/W, Santa Fe B/W. The latest dendro-dates at the former are 1145 A.D., at the latter 1194 A.D. (Smiley, Stubbs, and Bannister, 1953: 22-23, 25-26). The extent of the Santa Fe B/W occupation at these two sites and the pertinence of the late dendro-dates to such occupations is, however, not known. Presumably these occupations are minor, as Wendorf and

Reed show no Coalition Period occupation of either site (Wendorf and Reed, 1955: Fig. 3).

The excavations by Stubbs and Stallings (1953) at Pindi disclosed a large pueblo formed during a number of sequent building periods. The pottery is divided into two main ceramic periods. The initial pueblo and possibly some of the earliest additions are associated with the first ceramic period. The painted pottery of this complex is characterized by a heavy preponderance (80-90 per cent) of Santa Fe B/W, accompanied by a small proportion of Wiyo B/W and a very limited amount of Galisteo B/W (Stubbs and Stallings, 1953: 15). Culinary vessels are evidently smeared-indented (Stubbs and Stallings, 1953: 56) in most cases. The Santa Fe B/W was "fully developed" at the beginning of the pueblo's occupation (Stubbs and Stallings, 1953: 2). Wiyo B/W evolved locally from Santa Fe B/W and is thought to have been manufactured from *ca.* 1300-1400 A.D. (Stubbs and Stallings, 1953: 50, Fig. 70). Galisteo B/W is another local development, evolved from Mesa Verde B/W. Indeed "early Galisteo B/W" *is* Mesa Verde B/W; later sherds diverge from this type and are easily distinguished (Stubbs and Stallings, 1953: 15, 50).[2]

The original Pindi pueblo was built on a north-south ridge. It was a long, narrow, irregular building containing approximately 40 rooms, two to three rooms in depth. The structure is actually a multi-unit building, comprised of contiguous units of *ca.* ten rooms and an associated kiva. On the east (front) of the pueblo there were three (possibly four) subterranean circular kivas. In addition to these, two or three rectangular rooms within the pueblo were so constructed as to indicate that they were used for ceremonies[3]. Walls were of adobe. Fireplaces were found in the three rectangular ceremonial rooms and in one other room; they were not common (as suggested in Wendorf and Reed, 1955: 144; cf. Stubbs and Stallings, 1953: 31-32, site map).

A partial list of the artifacts from the first ceramic period deposits includes small side-notched projectile points; full-grooved axes of igneous rock (partially polished in most cases); numerous slab metates (one trough metate and one basin metate present); ornaments of turquoise,

2 A brief digression is in order, to explain this peculiar classificatory scheme. There is considerable evidence that some of the last peoples to abandon Mesa Verde, at *ca.* 1300 A.D., moved into the upper Rio Grande Valley. They continued to make their characteristic painted pottery, designated by archeologists as Mesa Verde B/W. With the passage of time, the pottery changed; i.e., it continued to evolve. Archeologists, rather than break the obvious continuum between "Mesa Verde B/W made in the Rio Grande Valley" and "evolved Mesa Verde B/W, also made in the Rio Grande Valley", applied the term "Galisteo B/W" to the complete sequence. The resultant difficulties are obvious; it will suffice here to note that any inferences of "intrusive Mesa Verde B/W" versus "local Galisteo B/W" must be examined critically.

3 Wendorf and Reed (1955: 146) apparently attribute all rectangular ceremonial rooms to later periods. Stubbs and Stallings do not assign the individual rooms to specific construction periods, but their room sections indicate that some of these specialized rooms may have been used by the inhabitants of the original pueblo (Stubbs and Stallings, 1953: Fig. 26, room 121; Fig. 27, room 138).

shell, and red shale; mammal leg-bone awls of types A-E; bird-bone awls, whistles, and beads; coiled and twilled basketry, represented by impressions on sherd exteriors; remains of corn and pumpkin. Turkeys were kept and apparently used for food in later periods of the pueblo. The turkey bone awls in the early pueblo may indicate the presence of domestic turkeys at this period also.

The earliest definite cutting date of wood from the first ceramic period deposits is 1246 A.D.; the latest is 1302 plus X (Stubbs and Stallings, 1953: Appendix B).

The absence of Wiyo B/W in the Santa Fe Component at Tesuque By-Pass suggests that the earliest Pindi Pueblo was occupied later than Tesuque By-Pass. This early period at Pindi, however, presents the only published information on a ceramic complex closely comparable to that of Tesuque By-Pass.

It is apparent that the Santa Fe Component at Tesuque By-Pass represents an early stage of Pueblo III in the upper Rio Grande Valley; nonceramic artifacts of this occupation cannot be isolated with any degree of certainty. Material from the earliest pueblo at Pindi, which may be slightly later, indicates several new developments, however, which foreshadow a great expansion in the upper Rio Grande Valley, an elaboraton of local carbon-painted pottery, the appearance of increasingly large pueblos, and the approaching dominance of the area in Pueblo history.

SUMMARY

Examination of data from other sites in the upper Rio Grande Valley indicates that the various components and occupations at Tesuque By-Pass are representative of more widely distributed cultural complexes in the region. The pit-house occupation in the Intermediate Area may provide an exception.

No definite evidence was found for a Puebloan occupation of the Rio Grande Valley north of White Rock Canyon and La Bajada Hill prior to 800 A.D.

The Red Mesa material from Area B is characteristic of a well-developed early Pueblo culture. Some elements of this complex are found in earlier sites located to the south, between Albuquerque and San Felipe Pueblo; others are found in sites to the north, near Taos. The total complex, however, appears to be characteristic of the area between Santa Fe and the mouth of the Chama River (Fig. 10). There is virtually no evidence that this culture originated within the upper Rio Grande Valley; apparently it was introduced by Puebloan immigrants from some other area, beginning at *ca.* 900 A.D.

Absence of data, both basic and comparative, does not permit a satisfactory interpretation of the pithouse occupation in the Intermediate Area. It is apparently pre-Kwahe'e, but there are no closely comparable sites in the immediate vicinity. A close architectural parallel was noted at an early site near Sandia Pueblo, but the comparison involves two rather irregular and poorly defined structures.

The Kwahe'e Component is typical of a period during which the earlier Pueblo complex (Red Mesa in Area B) changed and expanded. A number of new architectural forms appear, designs on painted pottery change, and corrugated culinary vessels begin to replace the earlier neck-banded forms. Occupation intensity is increased, particularly in the area from Galisteo Creek north to the Chama (Fig. 11). Evidence from several sites, and L.A. 835 in particular, indicates that these changes were rapid but continuous. It seems probable that there was both local population growth and continued immigration during this period. Most of these developments took place from 1100 to 1200 A.D. but probably began as early as 1050 A.D.

The Santa Fe Component, the latest occupation at Tesuque By-Pass, represents an early stage of upper Rio Grande Pueblo III. Pottery similar to that of the Santa Fe Component is found at many sites throughout most of the upper Rio Grande Valley (Fig. 12), but usually in association with other, later, kinds of pottery not found at Tesuque By-Pass. Santa Fe B/W is distinguished from the earlier indigenous painted pottery by its different kind of paint (carbon) and the addition of new design elements. Excavations at Pindi indicate other changes and additions in nonceramic traits during this general period. New architectural forms appear; side-notched projectile points, present in earlier periods, become the predominant type; slab metates are characteristic; grooved axes are common. Turkeys were probably kept for the first time as a source of food, and bird-bone artifacts become increasingly common.

The appearance of new traits, the evidence of continued population expansion, and the absence of information concerning transitional sites indicate the possibility of further immigration into the valley.

The rather unimpressive Santa Fe Component of Tesuque By-Pass stands at the beginning of a period during which Pueblo culture of the upper Rio Grande Valley was to undergo accelerated change, incorporating new people and new ideas, to reach its maximal development in the great pueblos of the Chama Valley, the Pajarito Plateau, the Pecos and Galisteo valleys, and the Albuquerque area.

DISTRIBUTION OF TESUQUE BY-PASS CERAMIC COMPLEXES

In the foregoing section, certain cultural developments in the valley of the upper Rio Grande were described with as few references as possible to neighboring areas. It was seen that the ceramic complexes of the Red Mesa, Kwahe'e, and Santa Fe Components at Tesuque By-Pass are characteristic of three major and consecutive periods of the early Puebloan sequence in a part of the upper Rio Grande Valley. In this chapter, the occurrence of these same and closely similar ceramic complexes in immediately adjacent areas is considered. Virtually all information pertinent to this discussion is derived from the pioneer surveys of the late H. P. Mera.

The Red Mesa ceramic complex of Area B is not widely distributed. The ubiquitous nature of Red Mesa B/W and neck-banded culinary vessels has been noted (see Fig. 13). The third element of this complex, "unidentified B/W," largely represents a local pottery style which is, in part, transitional between Red Mesa and Kwahe'e ceramic techniques. The persistence and continued development of this local style is characteristic of the Taos region ("Taos B/W"; Mera, 1935: 6), but in that area it is associated with a distinctive culinary tradition (Blumenschein, 1958: 108-9). Investigations west of the Rio Grande in the Chama Valley (Mera, 1935; Hibben, 1937) revealed no early Puebloan sites whatsoever. I know of no occurrence of Taos B/W or similar material on the Pajarito Plateau, in the vicinity of Santa Fe, or southward. Hence, the total ceramic complex of the Red Mesa Component at Tesuque By-Pass does not appear to extend beyond the Rio Grande Valley; it is to be found primarily on the east side of the river, between Santa Fe in the south and the Rio Chiquito in the north.

The ceramic complex of the Kwahe'e Component at Tesuque By-Pass is found both east and west of the Rio Grande Valley (Fig. 13). East of the Sangre de Cristo range there are several clusters of sites upon which are found Chaco 2 (Red Mesa B/W, as used here) and/or Kwahe'e B/W pottery (Mera, 1935: Map 1). These groups of sites, each centered on a western tributary of the Canadian drainage, are located along a line drawn from Raton, New Mexico, southwest through Las Vegas (Fig. 13).[4] From the northernmost of these sites (on the Vermejo River below Dawson) and from the southernmost sites (south of the Pecos River above Anton Chico) only Red Mesa B/W is reported. Both Red Mesa B/W and Kwahe'e B/W are reported

4 This line, incidentally, seems to mark the easternmost extension of Puebloan settlements in northeast New Mexico (Mera, 1935: 5).

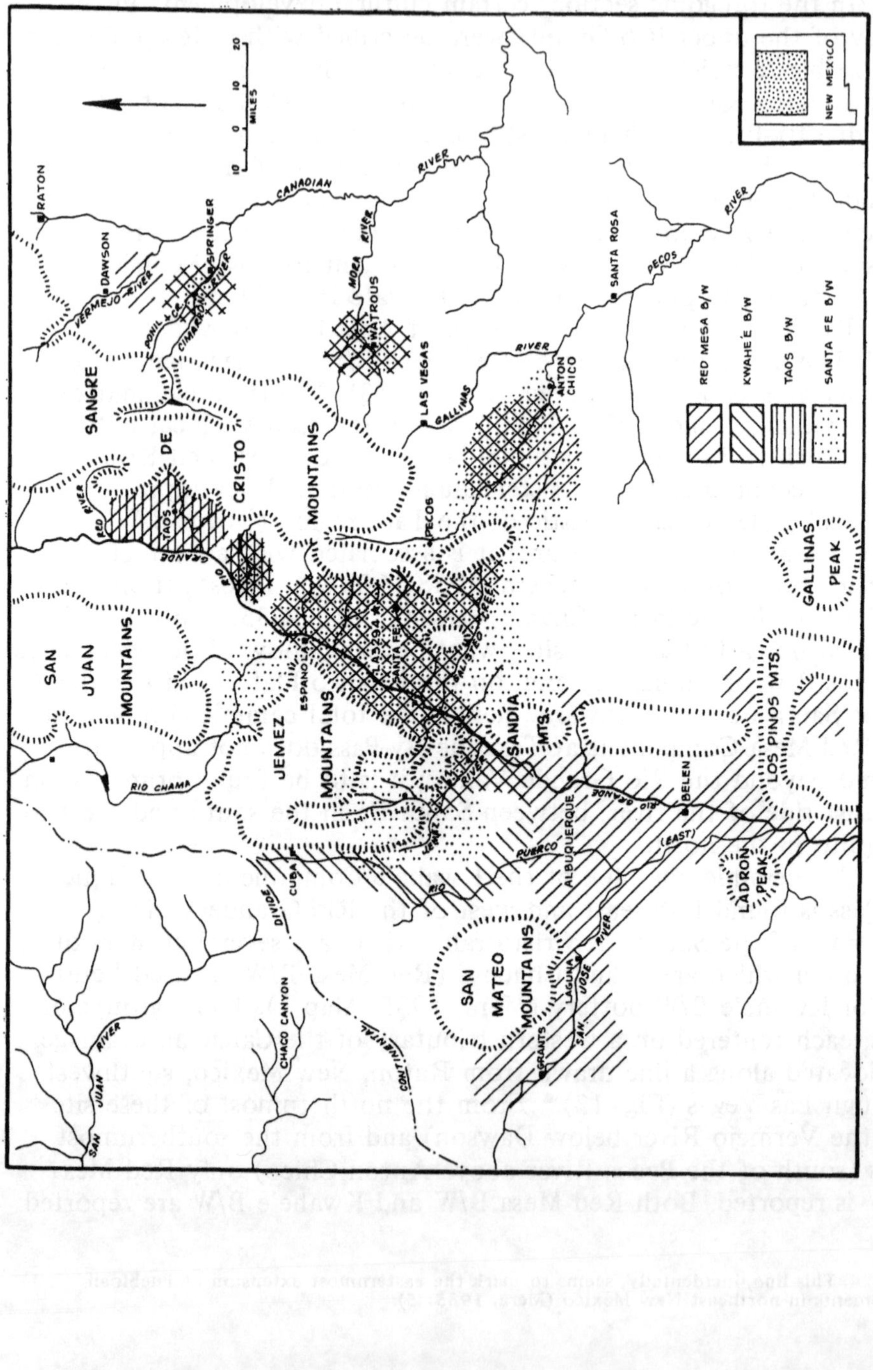

Figure 13 – Maximum distribution of decorated pottery types found at Tesuque By-Pass Site. Adapted from Mera, 1935.

from the Ponil Creek-Cimarron River area above Springer, from the Mora River in the vicinity of Watrous, and north of the Pecos River above Anton Chico. There has been virtually no excavation in this eastern area (cf. Lutes, 1959), but the absence of Kwahe'e B/W in the northern Vermejo River sites suggests initial Puebloan occupation or trade relationships characterized by Red Mesa B/W, and that Kwahe'e B/W was added to the ceramic complex at a slightly later date.

On the west side of the Rio Grande, there is no evidence of Kwahe'e B/W occupation in the Chama Valley or in the area to the north. Farther south, however, Kwahe'e B/W and Red Mesa B/W are found on both sides of the Jemez River west to Zia Pueblo (Mera, 1935: Map 1). Mera indicates a westward extension of Kwahe'e B/W from the vicinity of Corrales (north of Albuquerque) to the Rio Puerco (East), and thence northward up the Puerco to its headwaters, near Cuba. He reports no Red Mesa B/W from these sites on the upper Puerco however, and indicates that its distribution lies to the west, up the San Jose River past Laguna and Grants. Hence, the distribution of the total ceramic complex of the Kwahe'e Component seems to be: in the Rio Grande Valley from Corrales north to a point slightly beyond the mouth of the Chama, with extensions up the Jemez but not the Chama River; east of the Rio Grande in small enclaves on the Cimarron, Mora, and Pecos Rivers (Fig. 13).

Santa Fe B/W is apparently found east of the Sangre de Cristos in approximately the same areas as is Kwahe'e B/W (Mera, 1935: Maps 1, 2; Stubbs and Stallings, 1953: Fig. 69; but compare Wendorf and Reed, 1955: 144, " . . . along the tributaries of the Canadian, the potters retained the mineral paint tradition throughout the Coalition Period. . . ."). From the Pecos River sites, however, Santa Fe B/W extends both northwest to Pecos Pueblo and west past the south end of Glorieta Mesa to the Rio Grande (Fig. 13). West of the Rio Grande, Santa Fe B/W is found up the Chama and its tributary valleys to Abiquiu, throughout the northern and western reaches of the Jemez drainage, and still farther west to the vicinity of La Ventana on the Rio Puerco.

It has been observed that Santa Fe B/W is frequently found in company with later painted pottery and therefore it cannot be assumed that the total distribution of Santa Fe B/W necessarily reflects the spread of early and/or "pure" Santa Fe sites. Mera indicates that early (indeed, formative) sites are to be found in the Jemez drainage and west to the Puerco (Mera, 1935: 11-12). Occupations characterized by Santa Fe B/W unmixed with other types have been found in this area (Ellis, n.d.). In the Rio Grande Valley, relatively unmixed occupations are found at Pindi, possibly at Potsuwii II (Wendorf and Reed, 1955: 144), and, of course, at Tesuque By-Pass. Others are located on the Pajarito Plateau (site files; Laboratory of Anthropology, Santa Fe). Although the data are not specific, there is no indication of an extensive pre-Wiyo Santa Fe B/W occupation in the Chama Valley. There is, consequently, some indication that early Santa Fe B/W sites are found in the southern and central sections of its distribution, but not in its northern extension up the Chama Valley. Later sites, upon which Santa Fe B/W is found, occur throughout its area of distribution, with the possible exception of the enclaves east of the Sangre de Cristos.

SUMMARY

The specific ceramic complexes of the Red Mesa, Kwahe'e, and Santa Fe Components at Tesuque By-Pass are largely restricted to the valleys of the Rio Grande and its tributaries from the Jemez to the Chama, and to small groups of sites east of the Sangre de Cristo Mountains. Each complex is apparently distributed more widely than its predecessor. Major elements of each complex are found west of the valley, but not in the combinations characteristic of the Rio Grande area. The occurrence of apparently early Santa Fe complex sites on the upper Jemez and possibly west to the Puerco may provide an exception to this statement.

DISSIMILAR OCCUPATIONS WITHIN THE UPPER RIO GRANDE VALLEY

The "upper Rio Grande Valley" was originally described as extending from Isleta Pueblo in the south to the New Mexico-Colorado line in the north (footnote 1, chapter 1). Yet, in discussing sites comparable to the components at Tesuque By-Pass, reference has been made but rarely to those portions of the valley which lie north of the Chama or south of the Jemez Rivers. It is my purpose, in this section, to describe briefly the (Puebloan) cultural developments in these two widely separated regions, which will be referred to as the "Taos Area" and the "Albuquerque Area," respectively.

THE TAOS AREA

There is no evidence for intensive occupation of the San Luis Valley in Colorado or of the Rio Grande Valley in northernmost New Mexico (Renaud, 1942, 1943), and Puebloan occupation of the Taos area does not extend beyond Red River, about twenty miles north of Taos Pueblo.

Mera observes that the progressive deterioration of slipping techniques which characterizes the painted pottery of the Tesuque area in post-Chaco 2 times (e.g., Kwahe'e B/W) did not take place in the Taos area. On the contrary, the latter region was unusual in that its potters adhered to the use of a carefully applied slip "until the end" (Mera, 1935: 6-7). A divergence from the designs of Chaco 2 pottery did take place, which apparently paralleled that of the more southern potteries. The name "Taos B/W," was applied to this northern pottery type (Mera, 1935: 7). Regarding the appearance of Santa Fe B/W in the Rio Grande Valley, the same author observes that it was not adopted in the Taos area. Taos B/W remained in use "practically unchanged" not only during the spread of Santa Fe B/W "but also through a number of the evolutionary changes of the latter." (Mera, 1935: 8). The continued use of well-slipped mineral-painted pottery throughout the prehistoric Puebloan occupation of the Taos area is also noted by Wendorf and Reed (1955: 144).

The rectangular and circular pithouses of this region (Blumenschein, 1956, 1958) have been described. It was observed that the associated ceramic complex consisted of plain and incised culinary vessels, with a few, presumably intrusive, sherds of "P I-P II Chacoan types" dated 1000 to 1150 A.D., and possibly a few sherds of Taos B/W. In contrast to the Santa Fe-Tesuque region and the Puebloan area in general, the architectural and ceramic complexes of these sites are quite distinctive. This is particularly true with regard to pottery.

Blumenschein (1958: 110-11) also reports the presence of "numerous P II unit-type pueblo ruins" in the Taos area, and occasional P III manifestations. The painted pottery associated with the Pueblo II structures is evidently a variety of Taos B/W. Of a Pueblo III site north of Ranchos de Taos, with superimposed two-story house blocks, it is said "Taos Black-on-white was the dominant pottery in the lower level, with Santa Fe Black-on-white showing an increasing percentage in the upper" (Blumenschein, 1956: 56).

In 1920, Jeançon (1929) excavated a small pueblo just south of Ranchos de Taos, near Llano (cf. L.A. 1892, "Jeançon's Site" in Smiley, Stubbs, and Bannister, 1953: 38). Jeançon, of course, did not employ Mera's later type terminology, but the painted pottery from this site has been described as Taos B/W, Santa Fe B/W, and Taos Incised (Smiley, Stubbs, and Bannister, 1953). Wendorf and Reed, however, note that "the decorated pottery at the Llano Site was similar to that found in the same area during the Developmental Period [i.e., Taos B/W and Chaco II or Red Mesa B/W]. The designs were primarily Chaco-related hatched elements executed in a mineral paint. In the culinary pottery incising was frequently used, often in imitation of neck-banding" (Wendorf and Reed, 1955: 148). There is no reference to carbon-painted Santa Fe B/W.

The site which Jeançon excavated was a small pueblo enclosing a small, roughly square, plaza. Within this plaza, and occupying most of its area, there was a single circular subterranean kiva (Jeançon, 1929: 10, Fig. 2). This pueblo was constructed upon the debris of an earlier one, the walls of which were encountered during the excavations, but were not traced.

Jeançon excavated at several sites in the Taos area during 1920, and it is sometimes impossible to determine which sites his artifact descriptions pertain to. It seems, however, that both slab and trough metates were found at the Llano pueblo and that projectile points were typically side-notched (Jeançon, 1929: 17; Pl. 6 a, b; Pl. 9). No axes were found.

Concerning pottery, Jeançon observes that, although corrugated sherds occurred in abundance on the surface, none came from the ruin. Culinary vessels were coiled, then wiped with a corncob or some other rough object, and frequently incised (horizontally) about their upper portions (Jeançon, 1929: 20, Pl. 12). In the Taos region, Jeançon observes, "fully one-third of the sherds are a very good white with jet black decorations" (Jeançon, 1929: 21). He also notes that the slip tends to crackle or craze upon exposure to the elements, since buried sherds do not have a crazed slip although sherds on the surface do. Bowls are decorated on their exterior surface as frequently as they are on their interior. Although many of the sherds illustrated (Jeançon, 1929: Pl. 14) are apparently Taos B/W, a number of his design elements (Jeançon, 1929: Figs. 8-10, 11 *a, b, c, d*) do not conform to those described for this pottery.

Although one cannot be certain at all times of the particular site being discussed by Jeançon, the references to crazed slips, exterior decoration of bowls, interlocking frets and other designs indicate that the statement of Wendorf and Reed, quoted above, presents an oversimplification of the ceramic complex. On the other hand, crazed slip (characteristic of, but not restricted to, Galisteo B/W) and exterior bowl decoration (associated in the Rio Grande Valley most commonly with Biscuit B) are not characteristic of the Santa Fe B/W mentioned by Smiley, Stubbs, and Bannister. It seems best to conclude that the ceramic complex at the Llano site consisted, as stated by the latter authors, of Taos B/W, Santa Fe B/W, Taos Incised, and probably some other kinds of decorated pottery, transitional between Taos B/W and Santa Fe B/W and/or representing ceramic trends which postdate the appearance of Santa Fe B/W. No definite (cutting) dendro-dates have been determined for this occupation; presumably the series of dates from 1207 plus-1239 A.D. (no cutting dates; Smiley, Stubbs, and Bannister, 1953: 38) is derived from this pueblo.

This must conclude the discussion of excavated sites in the Taos area. Blumenschein (1958: 110) feels that, on the basis of intrusive sherds found on sites in this area, the following chronology applies to the Taos region:

	beginning date	end date
Pueblo I	950 A.D.	. . .
Pueblo II	1100 A.D.	1200 A.D.
Pueblo III	. . .	1350 A.D.

The end date for Pueblo III marks either a temporary abandonment of this area by all Puebloans or their permanent retraction into the immediate area of present-day Taos and Picuris pueblos. It is of interest to note Stubbs' statement that the site of Picuris Pueblo has been occupied "at least since 1200" (Stubbs, 1950: 27).

Before summarizing such information as is available from the Taos area, it is convenient to present data from perhaps the only sizeable excavation in any of the Puebloan enclaves east of the Sangre de Cristos. The presence of Red Mesa B/W, Kwahe'e B/W, and probably Santa Fe B/W has been noted in the Ponil Creek-Cimarron River area (Fig. 13), northeast across the mountains from Taos. Lutes (1959) has recently described excavations in the north Ponil region which disclosed Puebloan architectural features such as rectangular rooms with slab-based and adobe walls, adobe-rimmed hearths with deflectors, and jacal, in association with a ceramic complex composed primarily of unpainted pottery, an extensive inventory of stone artifacts, and much animal-bone refuse.

The apparent absence of cranial deformation, stone axes, kivas, squash, and beans; the small proportion of painted pottery; and the well-developed hunting complex which has elements in common with nonceramic occupations in this area, lead Lutes to conclude that "Altogether, it seems doubtful that the main roots of this culture lie in the Rio Grande" (Lutes, 1959: 67). The unpainted pottery at this site is described as

> sand-tempered and generally of a soft, friable, blackish or (less frequently) reddish paste. . . . Incised and punctated designs were found separately and together on 10% of the unpainted sherds. Incised designs usually were a series of horizontal lines on

the upper portions of vessels, while punctate decoration was . . . in herring-bone patterns on vessel necks. Other surface treatments were: banded - 9 sherds; washboard corrugated - 2 sherds; plain - 295 sherds [Lutes, 1959: 62].

Of a total 377 sherds, only 20 were painted, the majority of which were Kwahe'e B/W and Taos B/W. This ceramic complex has a great deal in common with that described by Blumenschein (1958) for the Taos pit houses, differing primarily in that the latter collection shows a higher incidence of incising.

SUMMARY

The Taos Area was apparently occupied by pottery-making peoples at approximately 950 A.D. Both rectangular and circular subterranean structures were constructed during this early period.

Throughout the prehistoric occupation of the area, a distinctive tradition of culinary vessel decoration was maintained. Horizontally incised, punctated, and (corncob?) scored vessels were popular; neckbanded and corrugated vessels were not. (This same culinary tradition is found in one of the northeasternmost of the ceramic enclaves in New Mexico, east of the Sangre de Cristos.) Painted pottery, particularly during the earlier occupations, was primarily a local development of Chaco 2-Red Mesa B/W ceramic techniques. The use of heavy white slip and mineral paint was continued in the Taos area long after they were discarded or replaced in the remainder of the upper Rio Grande Valley. There was, however, some penetration of Santa Fe B/W, and possibly later types of carbon painted pottery, into the southern part of this area during the post-1200 A.D. period. Apparently these types never became common in this region.

The Taos area was either temporarily abandoned by Puebloan peoples about 1350 A.D., or else the population withdrew to the present locations of Taos and Picuris Pueblos.

THE ALBUQUERQUE AREA

The presence of early sites in the areas of Tijeras Canyon, Sandia Pueblo, Zia Pueblo, Santa Ana Pueblo, and San Felipe Pueblo has been mentioned. With these exceptions, I find no other excavation reports pertaining to the BM III, P I, P II, and early (unmixed Santa Fe B/W) P III occupation of the area south of the Jemez drainage, west of the Pecos, north of Isleta Pueblo, and east of the Puerco. There has been virtually no other excavation of early sites in the area. Just north of Albuquerque, a circular subterranean structure with an antechamber, possibly BM III, has been excavated (F. H. Ellis, personal communication) and Dawson has recently surveyed the valley of the Rio Puerco west of Albuquerque (Dawson, personal communicaton).

Information regarding the early Puebloan sequence in the Albuquerque Area, then, is severely limited, particularly so in its southern section. Before considering the excavated sites in the region, I turn, inevitably, to the surveys of H. P. Mera, to present an outline of the ceramic developments which apparently took place in this and adjacent areas.

The early black-on-white pottery in the Albuquerque Area is described by Mera as Chaco 1 and Chaco 2 black-on-white. This is the same painted pottery which is found on the early Puebloan sites north to La Bajada Hill, beyond which only Chaco 2 (Red Mesa B/W) seems to be represented. From Albuquerque south past Isleta to the vicinity of Socorro, small sites with Chaco 1 (occasional sherds only) and Chaco 2 B/W are found in the Rio Grande Valley, in the East Puerco Valley to the west, and on the highlands which separate the two rivers. Extensions of this pottery east of the Rio Grande Valley, and particularly of Red Mesa B/W, are found below the Manzano Mountains.

Still farther south in the Rio Grande Valley, between Socorro and Hot Springs (Truth or Consequences), Mera distinguished another early (BM III-P I) black-on-white pottery, which he designated San Marcial B/W (Mera, 1935: 25-26). Subsequent surveys have located varieties of San Marcial B/W to the north in the upper Jornada del Muerto, the Rio Salado drainage (site files, Laboratory of Anthropology, Santa Fe), still farther north in the Puerco Valley (Dawson, personal communication), and in the Jemez drainage (Allen and McNutt, 1955; Vytlacil and Brodie, 1958).

Throughout the greatest part of this region, however, this early black-on-white pottery (San Marcial) is associated with a plain brown culinary ware. Brown culinary pottery is characteristic of southern New Mexico in general (cf. Mera, 1943; Wheat, 1955). In the Rio Grande Valley, the transition zone between the southern brownware and the more northern gray paste pottery is between Albuquerque and Isleta Pueblo; Mera uses the 35th degree of latitude as a boundary (Mera, 1935: 1, 24-26; cf. Danson, 1957: 101-2).

Following the Chaco 2-Red Mesa B/W period, the next major ceramic development to affect the Albuquerque Area was the appearance of a thinly-slipped black-on-white pottery characterized by hatchure, some broad-line designs, and arrangements of opposed hatched and solid figures. This pottery, Socorro B/W, is found not only throughout the Albuquerque Area south of Corrales, but west to Grants and south from Laguna to the Rio Salado.

Throughout its area of distribution, Socorro B/W is associated with a distinctive brownware bowl. The vessels were formed by very thin, overlapping coils, about .06 to .07 in. thick. Coils were not obliterated on the upper exterior surface of the bowl, but were allowed to remain as prominent ridges. Vertical and diagonal lines of punctates were commonly superimposed upon the ridges. The interior of the bowl was carefully smoothed and subsequently smudged. Mera designated this vessel type Los Lunas Smudged. Other brownware forms, primarily jars, are found, exhibiting a variety of surface manipulations, such as narrow neck-banding, neck-ribs, occasional corrugation and punctates used in combination with banding or ribs.

During the development of the Socorro B/W-Los Lunas Smudged complex, the people east of the Rio Grande apparently continued to produce varieties of Red Mesa B/W. In the Albuquerque Area, the Socorro-Los Lunas pottery seems to have remained in style during the greater part of the period with which we are concerned. Late P III sites in the area show rather heterogeneous black-on-white types related to both Socorro B/W and Mesa Verde B/W, associated with an early type of glaze pottery (Los Padillas Glaze Polychrome; Mera, 1935: 31-33).

Throughout the greater part of this period, however, the southern Albuquerque Area has its strongest ceramic affinities with areas to the west and southwest (see also Reed, 1955) rather than with the Rio Grande Valley to the north.

Excavations in the Albuquerque Area have, as has been noted, disclosed a number of early sites in the region from Albuquerque north to a point slightly beyond the confluence of the Jemez River and the Rio Grande. These sites will now be considered in some detail, not only because they provide our only data from this area but also because they are pertinent to an understanding of the early Pueblo occupations of the regions to the north.

At the Tijeras Canyon site (Wendorf, n.d.) a circular semi-subterranean structure was found with a ventilator on its east side. Construction features include four roof support posts set a short distance in from the wall, a deflector resting in a prepared socket in front of the ventilator opening, and pole-reinforced walls (Wendorf, 1953: 51). It is noted that "A firepit was probably present, but was destroyed during the excavation" (Wendorf, 1953: 51). Early painted pottery, classified as White Mound and Red Mesa B/W, and brownware culinary vessels were associated with this structure (Wendorf, n.d.; 1953: 51). Later sherds (Galisteo and Santa Fe B/W) were also found at the site, probably representing a later occupation.

In the vicinity of Sandia Pueblo, Peckham (1957) excavated three sites in which Red Meas B/W was the dominant painted pottery. At each site, L.A. 3289, 3290, and 3291, semi-subterranean structures were found. Small, roughly rectangular surface rooms were located at L.A. 3289 and L.A. 3290.

At Site L.A. 3289, the great majority of the unpainted pottery is classified as Lino Gray, the smooth-surface gray culinary pottery characteristic of Basketmaker III. Neck-banded sherds (Kana-a Gray) are present, but in small numbers (Peckham, 1957: Fig. 27)[5] In addition to Red Mesa B/W, other painted pottery, classified as Lino B/G and Kiaṭuthlanna B/W, was recovered from the excavations as minor types. These latter are considered characteristic of Basketmaker III and Pueblo I ceramic complexes, respectively. Decorated pottery types found (only) on the surface vary from La Plata B/W through the Tewa series, representing all stages from Basketmaker III through Pueblo IV. The various surface finds are few in number, and the late sherds are doubtlessly intrusive (Peckham, 1957: 57).

Peckham feels that there are two occupations represented at this site, Basketmaker III and Pueblo I (1957: 67 ff.). This interpretation is apparently based upon the presence of two distinctive architectural styles, a shallow squarish house with a short, wide lateral annex or entry on the west, four-post roof support, and a central hearth (interpreted as Basketmaker III) and a deeper, circular structure with a ventilator on its eastern side, four-post roof support, central hearth and ashpit, sipapu, and ladder sockets (interpreted as Pueblo I). The differences in the pottery associated with the two structures are very slight, however, and even these are not entirely consistent with this interpretation.

Projectile points (all surface finds) were typically of obsidian, small, with a triangular blade, corner-notches forming an expanding stem narrower than the blade, and a convex base. A single metate was found; it was troughed, with one end open. Two manos with a single grinding surface were found. Other artifacts are primarily chipped stone forms. It should be noted that the total artifact inventory from this site is small.

L.A. 3290 is located approximately 700 feet from the site just discussed. The major elements in the ceramic complex are Lino Gray,

5 No distinction is made between rim sherds and body sherds of Lino Gray. It is important for the reader to understand that Lino Gray ("Basketmaker III") and Kana-a Gray ("Pueblo I") are distinctive only in surface treatment of the neck area. Body sherds of the two types are indistinguishable, and many of the Lino Gray sherds from the Sandia sites doubtlessly represent lower portions of neckbanded (Kana-a) vessels. For another example of this unsatisfactory practice, see Allen and McNutt, 1955.

Kana-a Gray, Alma Plain, and Red Mesa B/W. Lino Gray comprises a much smaller proportion of the total collection than at L.A. 3289; Kana-a Gray (neck-banded), Alma Plain, and Red Mesa B/W are present in much higher percentages.

Structures at this site are interpreted as Basketmaker III (Room 5, a shallow rectangular structure with a short stepped entry on its south side and apparently a four-post roof support); Pueblo I (Room 1, a deep circular structure with a ventilator on its east side, four-post roof support, central hearth and ashpit, sipapu, ladder holes, and a deflector; possibly Room 2, a shallow oval structure with poorly defined floor features) and possibly Pueblo I or early Pueblo II (Room 3, a deep, rounded-rectangular structure with a ventilator on its east side and floor features comparable to those of Room 1). In this interpretation, the Basketmaker-Pueblo stages are used as chronological periods and the inference is either of a long occupation involving only one or two structures at a time, or at least two periods of occupation at the site. Although this is quite possibly correct, it seems equally probable that but one relatively short occupation is represented. Any interpretation of these sites must be tentative, due to the small number of sherds present and to the fact that body sherds of Lino Gray and Kana-a Gray vessels cannot be separated.

Three pipes (conical cloud-blowers) were found at this site. Two, of stone, were associated with burials in Room 1, and one, of clay ("brownware"), was found in the fill of this same structure. Projectile points are small and triangular, with and without corner-notches. Several varieties of chipped stone scrapers were found; hammerstones, choppers, and cores were relatively abundant. No metates were found, but manos with one grinding surface were present. A small turquoise pendant was found on the surface. A splinter of bone was sharpened for use as an awl (Kidder's awl type E). Two beads, one of bird-bone and one of shell, were found on the surface. A shell gorget (*Haliotis* sp.) was associated with a burial in Room 1.

At L.A. 3291, located some 250 feet WNW of L.A. 3289, the major elements of the ceramic complex are Lino Gray, Kana-a Gray, and Red Mesa B/W. Proportions of Lino Gray and Red Mesa B/W are quite high, whereas the neck-banded Kana-a forms only about 10 per cent of the collection. Kiatuthlanna B/W and a worked sherd of Socorro B/W are present as intrusives.

There is evidently but one structure at this site, a semi-subterranean, roughly circular dwelling or kiva, with a ventilator on its southeast side, four-post roof support, central hearth and ashpit, sipapu, ladder sockets and pole-reinforced walls. This structure is interpreted as a Pueblo I pithouse.

Only six artifacts, other than unworked sherds, are reported. One of these is the worked sherd of Socorro B/W mentioned above. The only other diagnostic artifact is a relatively large point or knife, with slightly asymmetric, convex blade edges, corner-notches, and a short, slightly expanding stem.

On the west side of the Rio Grande, and in the vicinity of Zia Pueblo, two structures are reported by Vytlacil and Brodie (1958). The structures are roughly circular, semi-subterranean, with entries or ventilators on their southeast side. House I has a four-post roof support with the uprights set near the walls, a central hearth and ashpit, sipapu, and either ladder sockets or posts to support a deflector. House II has complicated and poorly defined floor features which include a central fire area, ladder sockets and/or deflector posts, and numerous small pits and depressions. Two floors were found in this structure. A bulbous passage on the southeast side of the structure seems to be quite definitely a ventilator shaft, although its shape is atypical. It is possible that the ventilator was associated with the upper floor only, and that it was made by remodelling a bulbous entrance which was associated with the lower floor.

The two structures are interpreted as different occupations, Pit House I was late Basketmaker III-early Pueblo I and Pit House II as late Pueblo I-early Pueblo II (Vytlacil and Brodie, 1958: 177, 183). The ceramic samples obtained from the structures are in accord with this interpretation.

A single neck-banded (Kana-a) vessel was found in Pit House I, and painted pottery is classified as Kiatuthlanna B/W, La Plata B/R, and San Marcial B/W. The latter two pottery types were recovered from the surface only.

Associated artifacts include a shallow basin metate, a tri-faceted two-handed mano, a bi-faced one-hand mano, and fragments of two corner-notched obsidian points. The tri-faceted mano implies the use of a trough metate.

The ceramic assemblage associated with Pit House II has a higher proportion of neck-banded (Kana-a) sherds, and Red Mesa B/W is the dominant painted pottery. Two floor levels were found in this structure, but the ceramic complex associated with the different floors is virtually identical. Intrusive painted pottery (all from the upper fill) is classified as Kiatuthlanna B/W, La Plata B/R, San Marcial B/W?, and Socorro B/W. In passing, the authors must be commended for their care in separating neck-banded (Kana-a) and plain (Lino) types on the basis of rims only, and for not assigning the plain body sherds to either category.

A pottery pipe fragment was associated with the lower floor of the structure. Three points are described as tanged and one is of San Pedro type (all from upper fill). Manos are tri-faceted (fill, upper floor), bi-faced (upper floor, lower floor), and single-faced (ventilator). No metates were found. A broken three-quarter grooved polished axe or maul was found in the fill and a full-grooved, basalt axe was found on the lower floor. Two turquoise pendants were found in the fill and a bead of the same material was found on the lower floor. Three bone awls were found in the upper fill, but no descriptive details are given. A single bone bead was recovered (lower floor), and beads of olivella shell (fill, ventilator) and seeds (fill) were also found.

Two other features were found during the excavations near Zia. One was a shallow basin, 6 to 7 in. deep, roughly circular with a diameter of 7 ft. 7 in. Its floor was unplastered and contained no other features. No pottery was found in this basin-shaped structure, and associated stone artifacts are not described in detail (cf. Vytlacil and Brodie, 1958: 178). A second structure, interpreted as an above-ground storage unit, is described as having a circular floor with a diameter of 4 ft. 6 in. No artifacts were associated with this feature.

In the vicinity of Santa Ana Pueblo, another early site is described by Allen and McNutt (1955). Here, in a small area, several hearths were found at or near surface level and two deeply buried, circular structures were discovered in bull-dozer cuts made by a construction crew.

The site is interpreted as representing a single BM III-P I occupation. The ceramic complex contained neck-banded and plain culinary vessels, and the major painted pottery is classified as San Marcial B/W. Unfortunately, the authors did not distinguish plain body sherds from plain rim sherds, but described both classes as *affinis Lino Gray*. My notes indicate that in the *affinis Lino Gray* series, twenty-two rim and neck sherds were found on the surface and two were found in Pit house 2.

The structures, interpreted as pit houses, were circular, with four-post roof supports, central hearths, ashpits, and lateral passages on their east sides. The latter are interpreted as entries, but it is possible that they were ventilators, as suggested by Wendorf (Wendorf and Reed, 1955: 139) and Peckham (1957: 69). Pit house 2 had, in addition to the above features, indications of pole-reinforced walls, and two holes in front of the ashpit which may represent auxiliary ashpits, ladder sockets, or deflector posts.

Almost no artifacts other than sherds were found. A cloud-blower pipe (clay) and a relatively large, tanged obsidian point with two notches in each blade edge were found in Pit house 2; a serrate obsidian point with corner-notches and a deeply concave base was found in one of the hearths.

Returning to the east side of the Rio Grande, an early site is described in the vicinity of San Felipe Pueblo by Peckham (1954). Here, portions of three very irregular and poorly defined structures, interpreted as surface rooms of jacal construction, were found near a deep circular structure with four-post roof support, central hearth and ashpit, sipapu, ladder socket, deflector, and a ventilator to the north. The latter is interpreted as a kiva, and the site is described as probably representing a single Pueblo I occupation.

The ceramic complex at this site presents certain problems, as noted by Peckham (1954: 51). Identified painted sherds come from a single vessel of atypical Red Mesa B/W, and were found on the kiva floor and in one of the surface rooms. Culinary vessels were represented by almost 900 sherds, all of which were plain surfaced and comparable to Lino Gray. No neck-banded sherds were recovered, although neck-banded vessels occur at other sites in the immediate vicinity associated with apparently earlier painted sherds (Peckham, 1954: 51).

Among the artifacts from the site were a simple triangular point, thumbnail scrapers, trough metates (one with one open end), uniface and bi-face manos. One of the bi-face manos is described as lens-shaped in cross section and notched (grooved?), and another is wedge-shaped in cross section.

SUMMARY

The Albuquerque Area was occupied by Puebloan groups fairly early with respect to the rest of the upper Rio Grande Valley. Some structures in this region have been interpreted as Basketmaker III, and may have been constructed by 700-800 A.D., if not earlier.

Each of the early sites in the northern part of the Albuquerque Area is distinctive in its total ceramic inventory, yet it is not possible to give an unequivocal interpretation of any one of them, or to demonstrate a relative temporal sequence for them. The major factor which contributes to these difficulties is the very small number of artifacts, ceramic and other, which can be associated positively with the structures concerned. There are, on the other hand, certain characteristics found at all or most of these small sites.

Approximately circular, semi-subterranean structures with lateral passages on their east or southeast sides and a four-post roof support are found at all sites except the one near San Felipe Pueblo. The latter had a ventilator on its north side. The shape of the structures is a flattened circle (D-shaped), rounded-rectangular, or circular. The lateral entries are, in many cases, ventilator tunnels; entry passages may be present at the sites near Zia and Santa Ana. Insofar as can be determined, all of these structures had centrally located hearths and an ashpit. Hearths are normally circular with a raised adobe rim, and ashpits are usually separate, unrimmed depressions in front of the hearth. Sipapus are usually found, and holes in front of the ashpit (ladder sockets and/or deflector supports?) are common. Pole-reinforced walls, sockets for ventilator-dampers, and a united hearth-ashpit complex occur, but are not common.

Pottery is predominantly gray paste ware with small percentages of mineral painted sherds. Neck-banded culinary vessels are present at all sites excepting the one near San Felipe and possibly the Tijeras Canyon site. Brownware is present at Tijeras Canyon, L.A. 3290, Santa Ana, L.A. 3289 and L.A. 3291, in order of decreasing representation.

Nonceramic artifacts from the sites have been discussed. The individual assemblages are too small to permit extensive comparison, but basin and trough metates and corner-notched projectile points seem to be characteristic.

It is of interest that the sites containing greater proportions of brownware are those at which uncommon architectural features, such as pole-reinforced walls, united hearth and ashpit, and sockets for ventilator-dampers are also to be found.

There are no excavated late Pueblo II nor early Pueblo III sites in the Albuquerque area, but surface surveys indicate that the central and southern parts of the region partake of changes in pottery manufacture characteristic of areas south and west of the upper Rio Grande Valley. The northern part of the Albuquerque area, in the vicinity of the Jemez River, shows ceramic affiliations with the Santa Fe and Tesuque regions to the north.

ORIGINS OF EARLY PUEBLOAN OCCUPATIONS IN THE UPPER RIO GRANDE VALLEY

The early Puebloan occupations of the upper Rio Grande Valley have been described. Allusions have been made to the appearance of new traits and to "possible immigrations." The discussion has now reached a stage where such eventualities may be examined more closely.

Before pursuing these matters further, it is appropriate that I state briefly my feelings about what J. O. Brew might call the use and abuse of migrations. Overly enthusiastic postulations of migration have been a part of prehistory since scholars first attempted to identify the Ten Lost Tribes. Some investigators may infer a migration on the basis of a single find; others deny the probability of migration unless the complete cultural inventory of the supposed immigrants can be duplicated by a reported discovery at a single spot in the presumed homeland. I do not feel that it is necessary, or even advisable to take a strong stand at either of these extremes. The discovery of a single item of exotic type does admit at least the possibility of a small group of people moving into, or passing through, an area. If, on the other hand, a completely foreign cultural complex, well-known from another region, is found in any area, a strong probability of immigration is established. Indeed, if such a hypothesis of migration can be corroborated by the association of distinctive skeletal remains, the probability of the migration will be established insofar as it is possible for the archeologist to do so.

The latter case, in which a "most probable" migration can be postulated, is dependent upon the existence of several factors, however, which are not necessarily characteristic of migrations as such. Specifically: (1) the migration must be rapid; (2) the peoples moving must remain intact as a social unit; (3) the immigrants must be able to continue their old way of life in their new location with no appreciable period of adjustment to a new environment; (4) the source of immigration must have been the subject of archeological investigation. If any one of these conditions is not fulfilled, I doubt seriously that the cultural complex of the immigrant colony will be duplicated by completely corresponding complexes reported for the homeland.

Rouse (1958) has recently summarized the more conservative approach to migration theories which, in my opinion, demands the existence of these conditions. In taking this position he is in excellent company, composed primarily of scholars who have either wearied of the numerous but undemonstrable mass movements postulated at one time or another, or who have witnessed the discredit of apparently well-founded theories of migration. There seems to be an explicit feeling, however, that migration is a second-class concept, that it should not be introduced at all unless it can be *demonstrated* that "some other hypothesis, such as independent invention or diffusion of traits, does not better fit the facts of the situation" (Rouse, 1958: 64). Caution should be an accepted policy in making any of the above inferences, and Rouse has set forth the specific reasons for caution toward migration inferences in an excellent manner. I still feel that migration is a very important interpretive concept, and that it should not be disregarded whenever it cannot be virtually proven.

In most situations, the archeologist can only regard migration as more or less probable, depending upon such data as are available. At present, there is no accepted way of ordering the probabilities of migrations postulated on the basis of different traits (e.g., ceramics vs. architecture) and the matter is admittedly subjective. It is with such "possible migrations," however, that students of the Rio Grande Valley must be concerned.

It is most probable that the earliest Puebloans in the northern Rio Grande Valley were immigrants from somewhere within the area south of Mesa Verde, west of the East Puerco, north of the Datil Mountains, and east of the Chuska-Lukachukai-Carrizo Mountains. This region, consisting of northwestern New Mexico and an extension into southwestern Colorado, corresponds roughly with the "Chaco-San Juan," and includes two climax areas of Pueblo culture: Chaco Canyon and Mesa Verde. The term "Chaco-San Juan" will be used in this discussion to designate the area just defined.

Early ceramic developments in the Chaco-San Juan present striking parallels to the Red Mesa B/W and Kwahe'e B/W pottery sequence of the northern Rio Grande Valley, with regard to vessel form, finishing techniques, paint type, and decorative motifs. Ceramic typology in the area is quite frankly in a state of great confusion (cf. Gladwin, 1945; Reed, 1958), but the pottery of which I speak has been classified at one time or another as Kiatuthlanna B/W, Red Mesa B/W, Escavada B/W, Gallup B/W, Chaco Transitional, Chaco II, and Mancos B/W.[6]

Throughout most of the Chaco-San Juan, carefully slipped pottery decorated with Red Mesa style designs in mineral paint can be found in late P I and/or early P II horizons. In the following period, the slip becomes poorer and hatchured design elements become prominent. During these changes, neck-banded culinary vessels were replaced by corrugated vessels. These ceramic developments have been characterized as late Pueblo I, Pueblo II, and early Pueblo III; they took place from approximately 800 to 1100 A.D. The parallel to the Red Mesa B/W-Kwahe'e B/W sequence in the Rio Grande Valley is obvious, and it seems equally apparent that the sequence is somewhat earlier in the Chaco-San Juan than in the latter area.

So far, so good. In the realm of architecture, the situation is somewhat less clear, although parallels to the early northern Rio Grande pit houses and kivas do exist.

The floor area of early (BM III, P I) pit houses in the Chaco-San Juan area is characteristically divided into two sections by a ridge or partition passing through the center of the house, usually just in front of a centrally located hearth. I have noted elsewhere (McNutt, n.d.) that this "winged hearth," usually accompanied by a ventilator, ashpit,

6 It is beyond the purpose of this paper and my own capability to resolve this confusion. It has arisen primarily because of: (1) lack of specific and distinctive pottery type descriptions; (2) inconsistent use of type names; (3) tendencies of some investigators to associate all hatchured designs with Chaco Canyon and the area to its west and south, and to apply "Chacoan" names to hatchured pottery in the San Juan and Mesa Verde areas; tendencies of others to associate coarse hatchure with the San Juan-Mesa Verde district and to apply non-Chacoan names to certain hatchured pottery in the Chaco Canyon area. See Hawley, 1936, Hawley, in Kluckhohn and Reiter, 1939, for descriptions and basic references to the pottery involved.

sipapu, and four-post roof support, is typically associated with mineral painted pottery during the period from about 400 A.D. until about 850 to 900 A.D. Sites characterized by these traits are culturally very homogeneous in contradistinction to contemporary, geographically peripheral, heterogeneous sites with carbon-painted pottery and usually lacking the winged-hearth. It is of particular interest to the present study that there is no indication whatsoever of the winged-hearth in the early sites of the Albuquerque area, or elsewhere in the Rio Grande Valley.

After the winged-hearth ceased to be a popular architectural form in the Chaco-San Juan area, peripheral benches and finally, by Pueblo III, pilasters were incorporated into sub-surface structures. I shall anticipate the discussion of later periods in the Rio Grande Valley to point out that neither benches nor pilasters ever gained lasting popularity in that area.

During the period in which winged-hearths were being abandoned and peripheral benches adopted, pit structures were built in the San Juan-Chaco which had neither of these characteristics. The remaining floor features (ventilator, ashpit, hearth, sipapu, four-post roof support) are those which have been found characteristic of the early Rio Grande structures. The adoption of peripheral benches evidently began soon after 750 A.D. in the Chaco-San Juan (cf. Judd, 1924: Fig. 2; Gladwin, 1945: Fig. 6, 43-45; Martin, 1939: 380, 495) and winged-hearths were abandoned by 900 A.D. (cf. Gladwin, 1945: 65; Roberts, 1939; Martin, 1939). Evidence of structures with neither of these features is best in the southern part of the Chaco-San Juan, where they are reported during Gladwin's late Kiatuthlanna phase and Red Mesa phase (cf. Gladwin, 1945: Figs. 12, 13, 15; Roberts, 1931: Fig. 11; Roberts, 1939). The only comparable example which I find in the northern Chaco-San Juan is an undated kiva in the Piedra area (Roberts, 1930: Fig. 8). It must be noted, however, that there is very little information available from the northern Chaco-San Juan concerning structures with building dates from 870 to 950 A.D. (cf. Martin, 1939; O'Bryan, 1950).

There is evidence, then, that structures roughly similar to the early circular pit houses and/or kivas of the northern Rio Grande Valley were built during the transition between Gladwin's (1945) Kiatuthlanna and Red Mesa phases, and between O'Bryan's (1950) Chapin Mesa and Mancos Mesa phases. I hasten to add that there is no evidence that these houses ever became a standardized architectural type in the Chaco-San Juan, and they show considerable variability as a class with regard to specific architectural features.

There has been virtually no speculation on the origin of the early pit structures of the northern Rio Grande Valley. Wendorf has said that they are "reminiscent of Basketmaker III-Pueblo I pit houses of the San Juan Anasazi" (1954: 208; Wendorf and Reed, 1955: 142-43). He does not specify the pit houses concerned, but the nearly omnipresent winged-hearth in the eastern (mineral-paint) San Juan Anasazi sites provides a uniform contrast to the early Rio Grande structures, particularly during Basketmaker III and early Pueblo I. Data given above do indicate that the early Rio Grande structures are similar to certain Pueblo I-Pueblo II structures of the Chaco-San Juan area.

Allen and McNutt (1955: 248) say that the Santa Ana structures "are characteristic of neither the Anasazi nor the Mogollon area, but show a marked blending of influences from both regions . . . would cause little surprise were they found in the region between Bear Ruin and White Mound . . . " These authors emphasize similarities to Bear Ruin because they feel that the lateral passages of the Santa Ana pit houses are entries rather than ventilator ducts. Ventilators, however, are more typically found on other Rio Grande structures, and a somewhat more northerly (i.e., Chaco-San Juan) derivation seems probable.

This discussion of pottery and architecture of the Chaco-San Juan area suggests the following hypothesis: the early Puebloan occupation of the upper Rio Grande Valley, as found at several sites in the northern Albuquerque area, was initiated by groups which left the Chaco-San Juan area after 750 A.D.

Ceramic similarities between the two areas are striking. The architectural similarities are less so, and it seems probable that the circular semi-subterranean structures characteristic of the Rio Grande Valley became standardized in that general region, although they have prototypes in the Chaco-San Juan. Recent surveys in the East Puerco Valley, west of Albuquerque (Dawson, personal communication), indicate a fairly concentrated occupation during P I-P II times, and it seems likely that the early Rio Grande sites may represent an extension of a Chaco-San Juan occupation in the East Puerco.

The major objections to this hypothesis will stem, I think, from the implication that the early Puebloan occupation of the northern Rio Grande Valley proper and areas to the east did not begin much before 800 A.D. The presence of San Marcial B/W in the central East Puerco Valley and at the site near Santa Ana is pertinent, for this pottery is regarded as a Basketmaker III product (Mera, 1935: 2). Although San Marcial B/W is not found in the northern Rio Grande Valley proper, it is said to be associated with the characteristic Rio Grande circular pit-structures near Santa Ana (Allen and McNutt, 1955). San Marcial B/W is very similar, with regard to surface treatment, paint type, design elements, and all other attributes, to White Mound

B/W, a late Basketmaker III type of the Chaco-San Juan (compare Mera, 1935: 25-26 and Allen and McNutt, 1955: 250 with Gladwin, 1945: 22-23; note also MacGregor, 1941: 350). Gladwin was able to date the end of his White Mound phase and the introduction of neck-banded (Pueblo I) culinary vessels *at White Mound* "at some time between 785 and 801, or possibly [*sic*] a few years later . . . " (Gladwin, 1945: 37). Adams (1949: 293) estimates that similar changes occur in Chaco Canyon about 740-777 A.D. If, as I strongly suspect, San Marcial B/W is a late local variant of White Mound B/W, these dates for terminal Basketmaker III in the southern Chaco-San Juan are in accord with the hypothesis just presented.

Before leaving the subject of the earliest occupations in the northern Rio Grande Valley, I would add that there are other interpretations of this material which are equally reasonable although slightly more involved. For example:

a) the San Marcial B/W and/or Red Mesa B/W found in the Rio Grande Valley may be the result of diffusion to previously nonceramic non-Anasazi peoples.

b) the characteristic house-type found in the northern Rio Grande Valley may have evolved earlier than 750 A.D., and represents either nonacceptance of the winged-hearth complex (which may have had religious connotation) by local residents (suggested by Allen and McNutt, 1955), or it may simply indicate that the winged-hearth was "lost" during an early (B M III) migration from the Chaco-San Juan.

When and if dates are obtained on the early circular structures of the northern Rio Grande Valley, some of these conflicts will be resolved. At present, I favor the hypothesis presented above.

After the early Puebloan occupation of the Albuquerque area, and the apparent spread northward of related (Red Mesa) complexes, the next major ceramic development in the northern Rio Grande was the appearance of Kwahe'e B/W. This occasion is marked by an apparent increase in the number of sites, particularly in the region north of Albuquerque.

Kwahe'e B/W, quite apparently manufactured in the northern Rio Grande Valley, has been referred to as a "decadent Chacoan pottery type" (Mera, 1935: 34); "a local variant of [the generalized Chaco I - II style]" (Stubbs, *in* Stubbs and Stallings, 1953: 154); "a poorly made local cognate of contemporary Chaco types" (Wendorf and Reed, 1955: 141). Although Stubbs' allusion is to a style found throughout the Chaco-San Juan, the other references imply a rather direct relationship to the Chaco Canyon area.

In contrast, Gladwin is dubious of major influences from Chaco to the Rio Grande Valley, and says specifically that Kwahe'e B/W resembles pottery of the Four Corners area more than it resembles Chacoan types (Gladwin, 1945: 146). Kidder declares that Kwahe'e B/W sherds "are to my mind not at all Chacoan, from the point of view of decoration. They seem, on the other hand, to resemble more closely a generalized Black-on-white of the northern San Juan . . . " (Kidder, 1936: 597). Judd is inclined to find origins of Chaco culture in general to the north (1954: 32-34), in the San Juan area.

It appears, then, that whereas the change from Red Mesa to Kwahe'e design styles is characteristic of developments throughout the Chaco-San Juan, the specific design changes in the upper Rio Grande have their closest parallel in the northern (San Juan) section of that area.

New architectural forms appearing in the northern Rio Grande Valley at this time are Great Kivas, sub-surface rectangular kivas, and at least one D-shaped kiva built within a room-block.

Great Kivas are a characteristic architectural form in the Chaco-San Juan area, and are reported from Basketmaker III through Pueblo III stages (see Brew, 1946; Hawley, 1950; Danson, 1957, for discussions).

Rectangular kivas, either surface or sub-surface, are not characteristic of the Chaco-San Juan area. Although it is not profitable to speculate at length upon the rectangular kivas at L.A. 835 until more detailed descriptions and plans are available, it may be observed that possibly comparable structures are found to the south and southwest in the Mogollon region (Wheat, 1955), in the Flagstaff district (Roberts, 1932), in Chaco Canyon (Pepper, 1920), in the Ackmen-Lowry area northwest of Mesa Verde (Martin, 1939), in the Gallina region (Hibben, 1948), in the Taos area (Blumenschein, 1958), and to the east in the Plains area (Strong, 1935).

Of particular interest to this study is the possibility of relationships between the rectangular kivas at L.A. 835 in the Tesuque Valley and the roughly contemporary rectangular pit houses in the Taos region. The minimal amount of information available at present does not even permit a satisfactory comparison between the rectangular structures of these two areas.

With regard to the derivations of the new ceremonial architectural forms in the northern Rio Grande Valley, it may be pertinent that both large circular structures (interpreted as Great Kivas or pit houses) and rectangular, subsurface structures (interpreted as kivas or pit houses) are found in the Mogollon area (Wheat, 1955), in the Chaco-Zuni district (Roberts, 1932), the Ackmen-Lowry region (Martin, 1939), and in the Governador and Gallina areas (Hall, 1944; Hibben, 1949).

The single D-shaped kiva at Tesuque By-Pass is probably a peculiarity of this site, and further discussion of this isolated example does not seem warranted at present.

In view of the increasing population, the changes in pottery decoration, and the appearance of new architectural forms, it seems reasonable to assume a continuing immigration into the northern Rio Grande Valley during the Kwahe'e period. The apparently uninterrupted change from Red Mesa B/W to Kwahe'e B/W at L.A. 835, the specific design treatment of the latter pottery, and the appearance of the Great Kiva all suggest that the greater part of the immigrants were from the northern Chaco-San Juan area. Such a hypothesis does not account too satisfactorily for the rectangular kivas, although roughly similar structures are reported sporadically from that area. Regardless of the latter structures, further immigration from the Chaco-San Juan seems quite probable.

In the Taos area, a highly distinctive tradition of culinary vessels is found. Although a majority of the vessels in this area are plain surfaced, there is a high incidence of horizontal incision and of herringbone punctation. Mera (1935: 4, 6) evidently feels that this culinary tradition is a local intensification of an early Chaco tradition. There is little evidence of incising in the Chaco area, and none of a culinary tradition comparable to that for the Taos area. Incision, when used, occurs most frequently on neck-banded and corrugated vessels, not as a primary decorative technique (cf. Pepper, 1920; Judd, 1954; Gladwin, 1945).

Wendorf and Reed (1955: 143) observe that "The occurrence of incised pottery among the Rio Grande Anasazi cannot be considered a persistence of an early Anasazi trait, since incising was not common among the San Juan Anasazi. Instead, this difference evidently reflects the peripheral position of the Rio Grande pueblos and their proximity to the followers of the incised ceramic tradition of the Plains and Mississippi Valley areas." It is possible that the incised ceramic complex of the Taos area may indicate more than proximity of Anasazi Puebloans to the western plains. Several points are pertinent: (1) this incised culinary tradition was concentrated in the Taos area and appears northeast across the Sangre de Cristos, (2) the Taos area was quite conservative in their ceramic traditions, (3) early sites in the

Taos area have very little painted pottery, and (4) the distribution of the major Puebloan pottery types (Santa Fe B/W, Wiyo B/W, Biscuit B/W) is, for the greater part, deflected from the Taos area into the Chama Valley. It appears most reasonable to assume that the original northern spread of Chaco-San Juan Anasazi culture up the Rio Grande Valley met, and was stopped by, non-Anasazi groups in the vicinity of Taos who possessed a ceramic complex comprised of what is referred to as "Taos culinary ware." These groups apparently adopted the early, carefully slipped Chaco-San Juan painted pottery and, later, many design elements of Kwahe'e B/W. The origins of the non-Anasazi ceramic complex remain to be determined, but they probably lie in the central or southern Plains area. The presence of square pit houses in the Taos area is compatible with such a speculation. The route by which this pottery reached the Taos area is even more obscure.

The final major change in ceramics and architecture with which we are here concerned is marked by carbon-painted Santa Fe B/W in the upper Rio Grande. With the appearance of this pottery, there is a further increase in the resident population, possibly further architectural innovations, and several changes in artifact types.

The Santa Fe period is currently felt to be a local development. Thus, Stubbs (Stubbs and Stallings, 1953: 48) says that "From present evidence, Kwahe'e appears to be ancestral to Santa Fe Black-on-white." Wendorf and Reed (1955: 144) say "It seems unlikely that this [the introduction of Santa Fe B/W] was caused by the movement to this area of any significant numbers of new immigrants, since there are no evident accompanying changes in other aspects of the Rio Grande Anasazi culture which could be attributed to a western source. The pigment change in this eastern Anasazi area was a reflection of the shift in the San Juan Anasazi from the mineral paint of early Chaco and Mesa Verde to the organic paint tradition of the west."

There is, however, certain evidence which indicates that the possibility of further immigration during this period should not be dismissed. First, there is the matter of what I consider to be a major and fairly rapid change in ceramic technology, the change from mineral to carbon paint. To describe this as a "reflection" of the similar change in the Chaco-San Juan implies either diffusion of this trait from the latter area or parallel evolution. Wendorf and Reed (1955: 144) cite O'Bryan (1950) as authority for their statement that "In the Mesa Verde area, organic pigments replaced mineral paints by A.D. 1050 or 1100. . . . " This terminal date supports the idea of belated diffusion of carbon paint to the Rio Grande Valley, since Santa Fe B/W does not appear much before 1200 A.D. I am unable to find this specific statement in the source mentioned however, and presumably the reference is to O'Bryan's *initial* date for the McElmo phase, which is characterized by carbon-painted pottery (O'Bryan, 1950: 109). O'Bryan presents evidence that Mancos B/W (mineral-painted) pottery was made later than 1150 A.D., if not until 1200 A.D., concurrently with carbon-painted McElmo B/W (O'Bryan, 1950: 26, Fig. 6).

The transition from mineral to carbon paint in the Mesa Verde area was a slow one, occupying the better part of two centuries. The intergradations between mineral-painted and carbon-painted pottery are so complex and subtle that some have questioned the validity of a type (McElmo B/W) to distinguish a pre-Mesa Verde B/W carbon-painted pottery (Reed, 1958: 102ff.). Recalling the similarities in design between Mancos and Kwahe'e pottery, it would seem that design similarities between Kwahe'e and Santa Fe B/W would be expected even if the latter pottery is derived from a San Juan (McElmo) source. In addition, there is "a pronounced design influence from the Mesa Verde" in Santa Fe B/W (Stubbs, in Stubbs and Stallings, 1953: 154), and, although Stubbs feels that Santa Fe B/W is a local development, he notes that this pottery is "indistinguishable from similar material found in the classic San Juan center or even further west" (Stubbs and Stallings, 1953: 48).

Mera (1935: 11-12) felt that Santa Fe B/W resulted from contact of the producers of Kwahe'e B/W in the East Puerco Valley with people from the Gallina area, where carbon paint was characteristic. According to this hypothesis, Santa Fe B/W subsequently spread down the Puerco, east below the Jemez Mountains and thence northward into the upper Rio Grande Valley. I would suggest an ultimate origin of Santa Fe B/W further to the northwest, in the San Juan area, and its subsequent entry into the Rio Grande Valley via the Puerco and Jemez Rivers, along the path suggested by Mera. If this is correct, Santa Fe B/W would bear the same relation to McElmo B/W (or carbon-painted Mancos B/W as the case may be) as Galisteo B/W bears to Mesa Verde B/W: the continuation and development of a San Juan ceramic tradition in the upper Rio Grande Valley after that tradition had died out in the homeland.

In addition to the increased population and the larger pueblos of the Santa Fe period, it has been observed that slab metates replace trough metates, side-notched points completely replace corner-notched types, the full-grooved partially polished axe appears, turkeys were kept, and bird-bone awls occur. Any or all of these events may simply be the result of changing times in the upper Rio Grande Valley, although none of them appear to be inevitable. On Mesa Verde, O'Bryan's Site 34 is of particular interest in this respect: slab metates, side-notched points, and full-grooved axes are characteristic (O'Bryan, 1950: 82, 83, 84), bird-bone awls occur and turkeys were kept (O'Bryan, 1950: 109). This site is of the McElmo phase, and, although no dendro-dates were obtained, O'Bryan believes that the site was occupied from approximately 1025-1200 A.D. (O'Bryan, 1950: 79).

There is yet another consideration which suggests that migration may have been the vehicle by which the new traits of the Santa Fe period reached the upper Rio Grande Valley. It is fairly well established that the *entire* Puebloan population of the eastern San Juan had moved southward by 1300 A.D. But the exodus began much earlier. There are few post-1200 A.D. dates of initial pueblo construction in this area (O'Bryan, 1950: 14), and at least one Mesa Verde group had moved south to Aztec Ruin by 1225 A.D. (Gladwin, 1945: 129). The record of dry years in the early 1200s (cf. Smiley, Stubbs, and Bannister, 1953: 50) is in accord with this theory, and the frequent association of Santa Fe B/W with Galisteo B/W (presumably a post-1300 A.D. Rio Grande variant of Mesa Verde B/W) may well be more than fortuitous.

This presentation of evidence for a migration from the San Juan area to account for developments associated with, and including, Santa Fe B/W has been set forth in a rather laborious manner, primarily because such a migration is not currently believed to have taken place. As is often the case, as a person develops the evidence for an "alternative hypothesis," he comes to regard it as more reasonable than any other hypothesis. I find myself in that situation. In any event, the possibility should receive serious consideration.

In closing this section, a note concerning religious architecture is in order. Although it must seem almost inevitable that this discussion turn to the Chaco-San Juan in search of origins for upper Rio Grande culture, one of the most characteristic features of late Chaco-San Juan architecture has received virtually no mention. Almost universally, the kivas of this area are equipped with pilasters. The virtual absence of this form of roof support in the upper Rio Grande would seem to argue against hypotheses of repeated immigration from the Chaco-San Juan. The only examples of pilasters of which I know are reported by Stubbs from L.A. 835, where one structure had roof supports set near, and braced to, the wall by the addition of adobe.

No kivas of the Galisteo period have been excavated; it is here that Rio Grande pilasters will be found if they are to be found at all. But in any event, they were *never* adopted into the Rio Grande architectural tradition, for they are absent from post-Galisteo sites such as Pecos and Te'ewi. Wendorf has emphasized and carefully documented the persistence of the small circular kiva in the Rio Grande Valley, which has its obvious prototype in the early structures of the Albuquerque area (1953; 1954; with Reed, 1955). He adds that any attempt at historical reconstruction or linguistic-archeologic correlation must be "necessarily confronted by the dissimilarities in kiva forms between sites in the two [Rio Grande and Chaco-San Juan] areas" (1953: 51).

I cannot explain the absence of pilasters in the Rio Grande area, either before or after the Mesa Verde-Galisteo period. It can be suggested that (1) the Chaco-San Juan immigrants arrived in small groups which exerted more influence in the technologic than religious sphere, (2) that the immigrants were quite adaptable with regard to ceremonial architecture, (3) that the Rio Grande kiva pattern was simply regarded as "the way you build a kiva in the Rio Grande Valley." These conjectures are hardly testable and by some standards non-scientific. There is, at least, an apparent analogy to this situation in the Rio Grande Tewa emigration of 1696 to found Hano, on the First (Hopi) Mesa. "The town has a plaza layout and the general appearance of other Hopi towns. The rectangular kiva has been adopted from the Hopi, and by all indications Hano is a Hopi village in everything except language" (Stubbs, 1950: 99-100, Pl. XXI, Fig. 23).

The absence of pilasters in Rio Grande kivas does not, in my opinion, negate the very considerable evidence for several immigrations into that area from the Chaco-San Juan. It does suggest, however, that no extremely large group entered the valley at any particular time, although their total impact upon the resident population was quite significant; that the "immigrations" were actually results of small social units drifting into the area rather than a planned and organized population movement.

III

DISCUSSION

SUMMARY

Excavations at Tesuque By-Pass Site, north of Santa Fe, New Mexico, disclosed three distinct Puebloan components (Red Mesa, Kwahe'e, and Santa Fe) and two pit house occupations which could neither be assigned to nor distinguished from the Red Mesa Component. Chronological limits for each component and occupation have been estimated, on the basis of ceramic typology, as:

Santa Fe Component	1200-1300 A.D.
Kwahe'e Component	1100-1200 A.D.
Red Mesa Component	950-1100 A.D.
Pit house Occupation, Area B	900-1100 A.D.
Pit house Occupation, Intermediate Area	900-1100 A.D.

Analysis of artifacts and architectural remains indicates that the components at the Tesuque By-Pass Site are characteristic of the central (Santa Fe-Tesuque) portion of the northern Rio Grande Valley, and that they represent three major sequential stages in the early Puebloan occupation of that region. An outline of early Puebloan cultural developments in the upper Rio Grande Valley is presented in the following pages. Rigorous definition of the cultural foci involved, in either McKern's (1939) or Colton's (1939) use of the term, must await information from the major sites of the period, such as Arroyo Negro and L.A. 835.

Comparison of the Tesuque By-Pass occupations to those of other areas suggests that, although some characterics (e.g., kiva types) may be local developments, each of the culture types represented at the site may have originated as a result of emigration by small groups from the Chaco-San Juan area to the upper Rio Grande Valley. The case for each of these migrations, or population drifts, has been presented and is summarized in the following section.

AN INTERPRETATION OF EARLY PUEBLOAN OCCUPATIONS IN THE UPPER RIO GRANDE VALLEY

Two summaries of northern Rio Grande prehistory have been written in recent years, and each has appeared, in slightly different form, on two occasions: Stubbs' version in Smiley, Stubbs and Bannister (1953) and in Stubbs and Stallings (1953); Wendorf's, in 1954 and in Wendorf and Reed (1955). The former are the result of many years' devotion to problems of Rio Grande prehistory, and few would challenge Kidder's (1958:42) reference to Stubbs' "unrivalled knowledge of New Mexican archaeology." The latter are concise presentations of tremendous amounts of data, documented in considerable detail, and are most comprehensive in scope. I urgently advise the reader that the following passages are supplementary to, but in no way supersede, the summaries of Stubbs and Wendorf. This is particularly necessary because I shall dwell at greatest length upon those interpretations not entertained and, in a few cases, expressly doubted by these authors, rather than upon points of agreement and the obviously reasonable alternate interpretations which they have presented.

Wendorf has suggested a series of period names and dates for the prehistory of this region. We are concerned in this discussion with his Rio Grande Developmental Period and the earlier part, or "Pindi stage," of the Rio Grande Coalition Period. In the following discussion, I shall substitute the term "colonization" for "developmental." My reasons for doing so are twofold, but not of such a nature that I would care to take an unbending stand against the latter term. First, it seems quite apparent that much of the "Developmental Period" culture was developed not in the Rio Grande Valley, but elsewhere. Use of the term "developmental" must lead, on occasion, to such qualifications as " . . . [most of this material] can be assigned to the early part of the 'Developmental Period' of the 'Rio Grande Anasazi'. . . . This is not to say that much of the material had its origins in the Rio Grande Valley" (Peckham, 1957: 70). To this effect, "Colonization" seems appropriate. In addition, Wendorf's "Developmental Period" corresponds roughly, but *not* completely, with Roberts' (1937) "Developmental Pueblo." The "Pindi stage" is referred to herein as "Early Pindi sub-period." This is not just a semantic nicety; only the earliest pueblo at Pindi is pertinent, and reference to a subperiod as a stage may lead to confusion. Finally, certain of the dates suggested by Wendorf have been changed slightly to conform with the interpretation which follows.

THE RIO GRANDE COLONIZATION PERIOD (*ca.* 750-1225 A.D.)

The initial Puebloan occupation of the northern Rio Grande Valley proper may have been no earlier than 750 A.D. At this time, small groups of people from the Chaco-San Juan area entered the valley near the south end of the Jemez Mountains. Their immediate derivation was probably from Anasazi settlements in the East Puerco Valley. There is little evidence that these immigrants had ever occupied Chaco Canyon itself; a homeland in the Four Corners area or on the eastern slopes of the Chuska Mountains is more probable.

These Anasazi groups were the first people with a specifically agricultural subsistence orientation in the upper Rio Grande Valley. Hunting game animals, such as deer and antelope, was an important factor of their economy. They built circular semi-subterranean structures which typically had ventilators on their east or southeast sides, a central adobe-rimmed hearth, a sipapu, a separate ashpit in front of the hearth, two or more post holes in front of the ashpit (ladder sockets and/or deflector supports) and a four-post roof support system. There were, of course, occasional variations in this architectural pattern, which included unrimmed hearths, a united hearth and ashpit, no sipapu (found), probably side entries, and pole-reinforced walls. Painted pottery, comparable to Kiatuthlanna and Red Mesa Black-on-white, was decorated in a generalized eastern P I-P II style; culinary vessels were both plain and neck-banded. Data concerning the nonceramic artifact assemblages of these sites are quite limited, but basin and trough metates, small corner-notched and simple triangular projectile points, clay and stone cloud-blowers, and olivella beads are reported. Evidence of trade relationships and limited architectural influence from Mogollon groups to the south is found at some, but not all, of these sites.

There is no evidence at present that any of these groups moved northward up the valley to the Santa Fe area before 800 A.D., nor is there evidence that many had moved to this region by 900 A.D. On the contrary, site surveys suggest that most of the early Puebloan groups remained in, or were deflected south of the East Puerco-Albuquerque area during this period. The apparent reticence of these people to occupy the favorable environment of the Pajarito and La Bajada plateaus is most easily accounted for by the hypothesis that the area was occupied by another group, presumably nonceramic and non-Anasazi. Others have speculated on such a possibility (Mera, 1935: 34; Kidder, 1931: 151), and Wendorf (1954) has summarized the few data on nonceramic finds which are available (see also Miller and Wendorf, 1958; Wendorf and Miller, 1959). Although definite evidence is lacking for a late nonceramic occupation of the Santa Fe area, Hibben's (1937) finds of nonceramic occupations in the Chama Valley, presumably accounting for the absence of early Pueblo occupation in that area, add considerable support to this hypothesis.

Eventually, about 900 A.D. or slightly earlier, the central section of the upper Rio Grande was opened to settlement, and Anasazi groups pushed north into the Santa Fe-Tesuque area, while others may have moved eastward past Glorieta Mesa, thence north along the eastern foothills of the Sangre de Cristos. The northward movement in the valley continued to a point near the confluence of the Chama and the Rio Grande. The Chama valley was occupied by nonceramic, non-Anasazi groups, possibly remnants of the original pre-Pueblo occupants, which prohibited further expansion in that direction; the more northerly portions of the Rio Grande Valley were occupied by non-Anasazi groups which made unpainted pottery. The latter adopted the painted Anasazi pottery and much of Anasazi architecture, but were not absorbed by the immigrant population.[7]

The early Rio Grande Anasazi colonies were augmented by additional groups from the Chaco-San Juan during the 11th and 12th centuries. These people evidently followed the earlier routes, down the East Puerco Valley, eastward below the Jemez Mountains, thence northward into the Santa Fe-Tesuque area, for there are still no indications that the Chama Pass was open to Anasazi traffic. It is of interest that these later immigrants were not deflected south of Albuquerque, nor did they choose to follow such a route. These groups, probably from the northern Chaco-San Juan, brought with them new styles of pottery decoration (hatchure), new architectural forms, and, above all, additional man power.

The previous discussion has, for reasons stated above, placed great emphasis upon evidences for migrations into the northern Rio Grande Valley. The reader will have been misled, however, if he regards the local settlements of this period as no more than crude imitations of Chaco-San Juan Anasazi or as a simple and poorly developed culture type with no distinctive attributes of its own.

7 Recent excavations in the vicinity of Taos and Picuris indicate that cultural exchanges between the southern Taos area and the Santa Fe-Tesuque area during Kwahe'e-Taos B/W times were more extensive than suggested in this monograph. Also, the northern distribution of Red Mesa B/W into the Taos area is probably less extensive than was formerly believed, the distribution of Santa Fe B/W into the Taos area somewhat more extensive. (The latter, happily, adds confirmation to the discussion of the Llano pueblo.)

Actually, this is very appropriate to the general hypotheses concerning the Taos area, which suggest that the original occupants of the Taos region were non-Anasazi and became, gradually, acculturated to the Puebloan way of life beginning *ca.* 900 A.D. or slightly later. A poor representation of Red Mesa B/W in the Taos area would indicate that the acculturative process might have begun a century or more later.

For additional data on the Taos area, an excellent summary of the local archeology, and a different interpretation of the occupations represented, see Peckham and Reed (1963).

During the period of colonization in the upper Rio Grande, a distinctive and relatively complex culture type evolved, as represented by the Red Mesa and Kwahe'e Components at Tesuque By-Pass and other sites. Painted pottery was made locally which showed, if not the excellence of the unrivalled late Chaco B/W, a competence and concern with decoration which compares favorably with the rest of the eastern Pueblo area. Neck-banded and corrugated culinary vessels were apparently quite serviceable, although rarely the subject of elaborate secondary modification, as were comparable vessels to the west and south. Considerable architectural sophistication is apparent. Building techniques relied heavily upon coursed adobe, but this was used in combination with stone to produce several styles of wall construction. Jacal surface structures and subsurface pit-structures were also built. Above-ground dwellings and storage rooms were constructed contiguously to form room-blocks of from ten to twenty or more units, and several room-blocks were often built at a single site. The characteristic kiva had the floor features of the earlier semi-subterranean structures in the Albuquerque area, with other innovations, such as pole-reinforced walls, gaining in popularity. Other ceremonial structures include Great Kivas, rectangular subsurface and rectangular surface kivas, and specialized ceremonial rooms within the room-blocks. The floor-features characteristic of the Rio Grande kiva took firm root during this period, and were never entirely replaced. The following trade relations were established: with the San Luis Valley (Renaud, 1942) and the Cuchara district (Renaud, 1943) of southern Colorado; with the Gallina area, as evidenced by intrusive pottery and suggested further by the subconical culinary vessels (Hibben, 1949) and tri-notched axes (Hibben, 1938) found in both areas; with the Chaco-San Juan area (on the basis of intrusive pottery); with the Mogollon area to the south (on the same basis). There is, it may be noted, no evidence of extensive trade with any of these areas which would suggest a lack of technological independence of the Rio Grande Pueblos. Presumably the local villages relied primarily upon food plants for subsistence, but there is considerable evidence that hunting was a very important part of the Rio Grande Valley economy.

During this period, characterized by the local manufacture of Kwahe'e B/W, Puebloan settlements increased in number and spread throughout the valley from the lower Jemez north to the Chama confluence. Others were either established or supplemented on the eastern slopes of the Sangre de Cristos, and the Santa Fe-Tesuque area became, to a limited extent, a source of cultural influences felt to the north (Taos area), northeast (Ponil), and south (in the middle Rio Grande Valley).

There is little evidence concerning occupations in the vicinity of Albuquerque and southward during this period, except that which has been derived from surface surveys. Such information as is available suggests that sites in this area were peripheral to cultural developments to the west, southwest, and south, and did not belong to the upper Rio Grande cultural area as such.

Although the concept "Pueblo II" has contributed more than its share of taxonomic difficulty (cf. Brew, 1946: 32ff.), its original definition provides an excellent, if concise, statement of current developments in this particular area: "The stage marked by widespread geographical extension of life in small villages; corrugation, often of elaborate technique, extended over the whole surface of cooking vessels" (Kidder, 1927). Although the parenthetical reference to elaborate corrugation is not particularly applicable, it is apparent that the Pueblo II stage can be isolated in the upper Rio Grande Valley, and that it is characteristic of this colonial period.

THE RIO GRANDE COALITION PERIOD
EARLY-PINDI SUB-PERIOD, (*ca.* 1200-1300 A.D.)

Developments of this period, represented by the earliest Santa Fe B/W ceramic phase at Pindi Pueblo and by the Santa Fe Component at Tesuque By-Pass, were to a large degree a continuation of earlier cultural traditions in the area. Indeed, the degree of continuity between the late Colonization and early Coalition periods suggests to some investigators that events of the latter era were almost completely of local origin (cf. Stubbs, *in* Stubbs and Stallings, 1953; Wendorf, *in* Wendorf and Reed, 1954). It seems likely, however, that certain important traits characteristic of this period were introduced by small groups of immigrants from the San Juan-Mesa Verde area, harbingers of the impending abandonment of that region and of the subsequent Galisteo period in the Rio Grande area.

In any case, carbon-painted pottery with similarities to both local and Mesa Verde designs replace the earlier mineral-painted Kwahe'e B/W, slab metates replace trough metates, side-notched projectile points complete their replacement of corner-notched points, full-grooved partially polished axes appear, and bird-bone awls occur for the first time, perhaps a correlative of the appearance of domestic turkeys. There is an increase in the size of pueblos, but many of the earlier architectural features and construction techniques are retained. Sites of this period are found throughout the area previously occupied by the producers of Kwahe'e B/W. There are further extensions of Santa Fe B/W into the Chama Valley, into the southernmost Taos area, and into the

Galisteo Basin. It remains to be determined if the latter expansions came early or late within this sub-period, or took place subsequent to it.

During this period, the Taos area was either abandoned by pottery-making groups or else the population became concentrated within the vicinities of present-day Taos and Picuris. This question is, in my opinion, of great importance to hypothetical linguistic-archeologic correlations. If it can be demonstrated that the conservative groups in the Taos area, apparently non-Anasazi in origin and with ceramic ties to the Ponil district, were indeed the founders of Taos and Picuris, much evidence would be adduced for the hypothesis of an early Tiwa dialect both in the northern part of the upper Rio Grande Valley and east of the mountains (cf. Wendorf and Reed, 1955).

With the establishment of the culture type associated with Santa Fe B/W pottery, the Puebloan occupation of the upper Rio Grande Valley was virtually complete, and the stage was set for the arrival of additional groups and new ideas which soon transformed this area into one of the major climax areas of Puebloan culture. The reader is referred to the summaries by Stubbs and by Wendorf for an outline of subsequent events, and also to the discussion by A. V. Kidder (1958).

IN CONCLUSION

This examination of early Puebloan occupations in the upper Rio Grande Valley has, predictably, raised more problems than it has resolved. It is, I feel, a sign of at least some progress if major problems within any sphere of investigation can be isolated. With this in mind, the following suggestions are offered.

1) The ritual cry for more data from excavated sites is particularly pertinent. One cannot help but be surprised at the very small number of early Puebloan sites which have been excavated in the upper Rio Grande area. They are practically untouched east of the Sangre de Cristos, although highly competent surveys were made more than two decades ago (Mera, 1935; Renaud, 1937). Discussions of relationships with the Plains and areas farther east can be no more than conjectural until some excavation is accomplished in the northeastern "Pueblo" and western "Plains" sites. It must be equally apparent that only a minimal amount of data is available for the upper valley itself, and almost none for areas to the south and immediately to the west.

Fortunately, more work *is* being done in this area. Current projects of the Wichita Foundation in the Taos area (Wendorf, 1958), the Atomic Energy Commission in the vicinity of Los Alamos (Worman, 1959), the Laboratory of Anthropology in the Santa Fe-Tesuque region, the University of New Mexico and its staff in the Jemez and Puerco drainages, the wide-ranging Highway Salvage Archaeology project, and work by the Philmont Scout Ranch east of the Sangre de Cristos will all add vital information to that presently available.

2) The very excellent dendrochronological studies (Smiley, Stubbs, and Bannister, 1953) initiated by the University of Arizona and Museum of New Mexico should, if at all possible, be continued. It would seem profitable to concentrate on relatively early sites (San Marcial B/W, Red Mesa B/W, Kwahe'e B/W, Taos B/W, Santa Fe B/W) with unmixed ceramic complexes, in each region of the upper valley. By this means, and possibly only by this means, many of the alternative interpretations of local prehistory will be resolved.

3) Both survey for and excavation of nonceramic sites in the upper Rio Grande and adjacent areas should be intensified. The beginnings of such work in the area have been most promising, and further data will be pertinent to an understanding of both Pueblo and non-Pueblo occupation of the area.

4) A *comparative* design analysis of local varieties of the generalized Chaco I-II or Pueblo I-II painted potteries (Mancos, McElmo, Red Mesa, Escavada, Gallup, Kwahe'e, Taos, etc., etc. B/W) should do much to resolve the many problems of taxonomy and interpretation that exist at present.

5) Culinary vessels of the area must be studied. There is every indication that, in this particular area, they are as sensitive to temporal and cultural change as are the painted vessels. In addition, it seems likely that chronological inferences based on culinary vessels will not merely duplicate those based upon painted pottery. Changes in culinary vessels apparently took place independently of shifts in painted designs, and they quite probably will provide bases for chronological inferences throughout the area. Finally, it is in the class of unpainted vessels that one can expect to find the greatest evidence for the penetration of non-Puebloan ceramic concepts into the upper Rio Grande area.

6) The absence of kiva pilasters poses a very interesting problem concerning Puebloan attitudes toward ceremonial architecture. Inter-pueblo relations in religious affairs have been documented in many ethnographic works. The present study poses several questions pertinent to these relationships. Specifically, how do various pueblos feel about changing particular architectural features in

their ceremonial structures? How do they feel about adopting new features? What is their attitude toward the adoption of local ceremonial structures by immigrant groups? Do any of these feelings differ by linguistic subgroups? Answers to these and related queries would be of considerable anthropological interest and would be of the greatest pertinence to current interpretations of Southwestern prehistory in general.

The above paragraph is not a request for obviously pertinent data which has been omitted from the ethnographic literature, thus frustrating the course of archeology. After all, there is no published data whatsoever on an excavated kiva from the Galisteo-Mesa Verde period in the upper Rio Grande Valley. The nonacceptance of pilasters in this area is a rather specialized situation, but it provides an excellent opportunity for the combination of archeological and ethnological techniques to resolve a specific anthropological problem.

7) In closing, a rather negative conclusion can be offered. The upper Rio Grande Valley, on the eastern periphery of the Puebloan region, is a likely area for contact between Southwestern and Plains peoples. During the period discussed in this paper, there is surprisingly little evidence of such contact.

The culinary pottery tradition in the Taos and Ponil districts possesses such Plains ceramic characteristics as horizontal incision and corncob scoring. These traits did not spread south from Taos down the Rio Grande Valley, although they may have passed westward to the Gallina area. The subconical, or contracted, vessel base of the Taos area is, however, characteristic of sites to the south (e.g., the neck-banded jars at Tesuque By-Pass Site and L.A. 835).

The grooved axes and side-notched projectile points of the southwestern and the eastern United States may be related in some manner (cf. Griffin, 1955; Wauchope, ed., 1956: 99-100), but the Rio Grande Anasazi apparently received these artifacts, as well as carbon-painted pottery, slab metates, and turkeys, from the Chaco-San Juan area at or slightly later than 1200 A.D. The *initial* diffusion of these artifacts between the Southwest and the eastern United States, if such indeed did occur, either passed through non-Anasazi peoples in the Rio Grande Valley, or not through that area at all.

REFERENCES CITED

Adams, Richard N.
1949 Half House: A Pithouse in Chaco Canyon, New Mexico. Papers of the Michigan Academy of Science, Arts, and Letters, Vol. XXXV, pp. 273-95. Ann Arbor.

Allen, J. W. and C. H. McNutt
1955 A Pit House Site near Santa Ana Pueblo, New Mexico. American Antiquity, Vol. 20, No. 3, pp. 241-55. Menasha.

Bailey, F. M.
1928 Birds of New Mexico. New Mexico Department of Game and Fish. Santa Fe.

Bailey, Vernon
1913 Life Zones and Crop Zones of New Mexico. North American Fauna, United States Department of Agriculture, Bureau of Biological Survey, No. 35. Washington, D. C.

1931 Mammals of New Mexico. North American Fauna, United States Department of Agriculture, Bureau of Biological Survey, No. 53. Washington, D. C.

Blumenschein, Helen
1956 Excavations in the Taos Area, 1953-1955. El Palacio, Vol. 63, No. 2, pp. 53-56. Santa Fe.

1958 Further Excavations and Surveys in the Taos Area. El Palacio, Vol. 65, No. 3, pp. 107-11. Santa Fe.

Brew, John Otis
1946 Archaeology of Alkalai Ridge, Southeastern Utah. Papers of the Peabody Museum of American Archaeology and Ethnology, Harvard University, Vol. XXI. Cambridge.

Colton, Harold S.
1939 Prehistoric Culture Units and their Relationships in Northern Arizona. Museum of Northern Arizona, Bulletin 17. Flagstaff.

1946 The Sinagua, a Summary of the Archaeology of the Region of Flagstaff, Arizona. Museum of Northern Arizona, Bulletin 22. Flagstaff.

Danson, Edward Bridge
1957 An Archaeological Survey of West Central New Mexico and East Central Arizona. Papers of the Peabody Museum of Archaeology and Ethnology, Harvard University, Vol XLIV, No. 1. Cambridge.

Ellis, Florence H.
n.d. Anthropological Evidence Supporting the Land Claim of the Pueblos of Zia, Santa Ana, and Jemez. Manuscript *ca.* 1957, University of New Mexico, Albuquerque.

Fenneman, Nevin M.
1931 Physiography of Western United States. McGraw-Hill Company. New York and London.

Gladwin, Harold Sterling
1945 The Chaco Branch; Excavations at White Mound and in the Red Mesa Valley. Medallion Papers, Gila Pueblo, No. XXXIII. Globe.

Gladwin, Winifred and Harold Sterling Gladwin
1934 A Method for Designation of Cultures and their Variations. Medallion Papers, Gila Pueblo, No. XV. Globe.

Griffin, James B.
1955 Observations on the Grooved Axe in North America. Pennsylvania Archaeologist, Vol. XXV, No. 1, pp. 31-43. Harrisburg.

Hall, Edward Twitchell, Jr.
1944 Early Stockaded Villages in the Governador, New Mexico. Columbia Studies in Archeology and Ethnology, Vol. II, Part 1. New York.

Hawley, Florence M.
1936 Field Manual of Prehistoric Southwestern Pottery Types. Anthropological Series, The University of New Mexico Bulletin, Vol. 1, No. 4. Albuquerque.
1950 Big Kivas, Little Kivas, and Moiety Houses in Historical Reconstruction. Southwestern Journal of Anthropology, Vol. 6, No. 3, pp. 286-302. Albuquerque.

Hewett, Edgar Lee
1953 Pajarito Plateau and its Ancient People (rev. Bertha P. Dutton). University of New Mexico Press. Albuquerque.

Hewett, Edgar Lee, Junius Henderson, and Wilfred W. Robbins
1913 The Physiography of the Rio Grande Valley, New Mexico, in Relation to Pueblo Culture. Bureau of American Ethnology, Smithsonian Institution, Bulletin 54. Washington, D. C.

Hibben, Frank C.
1937 Excavation of the Riana Ruin and Chama Valley Survey. Anthropological Series, The University of New Mexico Bulletin, Vol. 2, No. 1. Albuquerque.
1938 The Gallina Phase. American Antiquity, Vol. IV, No. 2, pp. 131-36. Menasha.
1948 The Gallina Architectural Forms. American Antiquity, Vol. XIV, No. 1, pp. 32-36. Menasha
1949 The Pottery of the Gallina Complex. American Antiquity, Vol. XIV, No. 3, pp. 194-202. Menasha.

Jeançon, J. A.
1929 Archeological Investigations in the Taos Valley, New Mexico, During 1920. Smithsonian Miscellaneous Collections, Vol. 81, No. 12. Baltimore.

Judd, Neil M.
1924 Two Chaco Canyon Pit Houses. Annual Report, 1922, Smithsonian Institution, pp. 399-413. Washington, D. C.
1954 The Material Culture of Pueblo Bonito. Smithsonian Miscellaneous Collections, Vol. 124. Baltimore.

Kidder, Alfred Vincent
1927 Southwestern Archaeological Conference. El Palacio, Vol. 23, No. 22, pp. 554-61. Santa Fe.
1931 The Pottery of Pecos, Volume I. Papers of the Southwestern Expedition, Phillips Academy, No. 5. New Haven.
1936 The Pottery of Pecos, Volume II. Papers of the Southwestern Expedition, Phillips Academy, No. 7. New Haven.
1958 Pecos, New Mexico: Archaeological Notes. Papers of the Robert S. Peabody Foundation for Archaeology, Vol. 5. Andover.

Kluckhohn, Clyde and Paul Reiter (eds.)
1939 Preliminary Report on the 1937 Excavations, Bc 50-51, Chaco Canyon, New Mexico. Anthropological Series, The University of New Mexico Bulletin, Vol. 3, No. 2. Albuquerque.

Lambert, Marjorie F.
1956 A Prehistoric Stone Elbow Pipe from the Taos Area. El Palacio, Vol. 63, No. 2 pp. 67-68. Santa Fe.

Luebben, Ralph A.
1953 Leaf Water Site. *In* Salvage Archaeology in the Chama Valley, New Mexico, compiled by Fred Wendorf. Monographs of the School of American Research. No. 17, pp. 9-33. Santa Fe.

Lutes, Eugene
1959 A Marginal Prehistoric Culture of Northeastern New Mexico. El Palacio, Vol. 66, No. 2, pp. 55-68. Santa Fe.

Mc Gregor, John C.
1941 Southwestern Archaeology. John Wiley and Sons, Inc. New York.

McKern, W. C.
1939 The Midwestern Taxonomic Method as an Aid to Archaeological Culture Study. American Antiquity, Vol. 4, No. 4, pp. 301-13. Menasha.

McNutt, Charles H.
n.d. A Re-evaluation of the San Juan Basket Maker Culture and Possible Relationships to Certain Non-ceramic Groups. 1954 Masters Thesis, Department of Anthropology, University of New Mexico. Albuquerque.

Martin, Paul S.
1939 Modified Basket Maker Sites, Ackmen-Lowry Area, Southwestern Colorado. Anthropological Series, Field Museum of Natural History, Vol. XXIII, No. 3, publication 444, pp. 307-497. Chicago.

Mera, H. P.
1935 Ceramic Clues to the Prehistory of North Central New Mexico. Technical Series, Laboratory of Anthropology, Bulletin No. 8. Santa Fe.

1943 An Outline of Ceramic Developments in Southern and Southeastern New Mexico. Technical Series, Laboratory of Anthropology, Bulletin No. 11. Santa Fe.

Miller, John P. and Fred Wendorf
1958 Alluvial Chronology of the Tesuque Valley, New Mexico. Journal of Geology, Vol. 66, No. 2, pp. 117-94. Chicago.

O'Bryan, Deric
1950 Excavations in Mesa Verde National Park, 1947-1948. Medallion Papers, Gila Pueblo, No. XXXIX. Globe.

Peckham, Stewart
1954 A Pueblo I Site near San Felipe Pueblo, New Mexico. Highway Salvage Archaeology, Vol. I, No. 4, pp. 41-51. Santa Fe.

1957 Three Pithouse Sites near Albuquerque, New Mexico. Highway Salvage Archaeology, Vol. III. pp. 39-70. Santa Fe.

Peckham, Stewart and Erik K. Reed
1963 Three Sites near Ranchos de Taos, New Mexico. Highway Salvage Archeology, Vol. IV, No. 15, pp. 1-28. Santa Fe.

Pepper, George H.
1920 Pueblo Bonito. Anthropological Papers, The American Museum of Natural History, Vol. XXVII. New York.

Reed, Erik K.
1942 Implications of the Mogollon Concept. American Antiquity, Vol. 8, No. 1, pp. 27-31. Menasha.

1955 Painted Pottery and Zuni History. Southwestern Journal of Anthropology, Vol. 11, No. 2, pp. 178-93. Albuquerque.

1957 Human Skeletal Remains from some Highway Salvage Excavations in New Mexico. Highway Salvage Archaeology, Vol. III. pp. 85-97. Santa Fe.

1958 Excavations in Mancos Canyon. Anthropological Papers, University of Utah, No. 35. Salt Lake.

Renaud, E. B.
1937 Northeastern New Mexico. The Archaeological Survey of the High Western Plains, University of Denver, Ninth Report. Denver.
1942 Reconnaissance Work in the Upper Rio Grande Valley, Colorado and New Mexico. Archaeological Series, University of Denver, Third Paper. Denver.
1943 Archaeological Sites of the Cuchara Drainage, Southern Colorado. Archaeological Series, University of Denver, Fourth Paper. Denver.

Reynolds, S. E.
1956 Climatological Summary, New Mexico. Technical Series, State of New Mexico, State Engineer Office, No. 5. Santa Fe.

Roberts, Frank H. H., Jr.
1930 Early Pueblo Ruins in the Piedra District, Southwestern Colorado. Bureau of American Ethnology, Smithsonian Institution, Bulletin 96. Washington, D. C.
1931 The Ruins at Kiatuthlanna, Eastern Arizona. Bureau of American Ethnology, Smithsonian Institution, Bulletin 100. Washington, D. C.
1932 The Village of the Great Kivas on the Zuni Reservation, New Mexico. Bureau of American Ethnology, Smithsonian Institution, Bulletin 111. Washington, D. C.
1937 Archeology in the Southwest. American Antiquity, Vol. 3, No. 1, pp. 3-33. Menasha.
1939 Archeological Remains in the Whitewater District, Eastern Arizona: Part I; House Types. Bureau of American Ethnology, Smithsonian Institution, Bulletin 121. Washington, D. C.

Rouse, Irving
1958 The Inference of Migrations from Anthropological Evidence. *In:* Migrations in New World Culture History, edited by R. H. Thompson. University of Arizona Social Science Bulletin, No. 27. Tucson.

Smiley, Terah L., Stanley A. Stubbs, and Bryant Bannister
1953 A Foundation for the Dating of some Late Archaeological Sites in the Rio Grande Area, New Mexico. Laboratory of Tree-Ring Research, University of Arizona, Bulletin No. 6. Tucson.

Strong, William Duncan
1935 An Introduction to Nebraska Archaeology. Smithsonian Miscellaneous Collections, Vol. 93, No. 10. Washington, D. C.

Stubbs, Stanley A.
1950 Bird's-Eye View of the Pueblos. University of Oklahoma Press. Norman.
1954 Summary Report on an Early Pueblo Site in the Tesuque Valley, New Mexico. El Palacio, Vol. 62, No. 2, pp. 43-45. Santa Fe.

Stubbs, Stanley A. and W. S. Stallings, Jr.
1953 The Excavation of Pindi Pueblo, New Mexico. Monographs of the School of American Research and the Laboratory of Anthropology, No. 18. Santa Fe.

Vytlacil, Natalie and J. J. Brodie
1958 Two Pit Houses near Zia Pueblo. El Palacio, Vol. 65, No. 5, pp. 174-84. Santa Fe.

Wauchope, Robert (ed.)
1956 Seminars in Archaeology: 1955. Memoirs of the Society for American Archaeology, No. 11. Salt Lake City.

Wendorf, Fred
1954 A Reconstruction of Northern Rio Grande Prehistory. American Anthropologist, Vol. 56, No. 2, Part 1, pp. 200-227. Menasha.
1958 Pot Creek Project: 1958 Season. El Palacio, Vol. 63, No. 4, p. 150. Santa Fe.
n.d. Account of excavations by Stubbs and Wendorf at L.A. 586, Tijeras Canyon, New Mexico. Manuscript, Department of Anthropology, University of New Mexico. Albuquerque.

Wendorf, Fred (comp.)
1953 Salvage Archaeology in the Chama Valley, New Mexico. Monographs of the School of American Research, No. 17. Santa Fe.

Wendorf, Fred, Nancy Fox, and Orian L. Lewis (eds.)
1956 Pipeline Archaeology. The Laboratory of Anthropology and the Museum of Northern Arizona. Santa Fe and Flagstaff.

Wendorf, Fred and John P. Miller
1959 Artifacts from High Mountain Sites in the Sangre de Cristo Range. El Palacio, Vol. 66, No. 2, pp. 37-52. Santa Fe.

Wendorf, Fred and Erik K. Reed
1955 An Alternative Reconstruction of Northern Rio Grande Prehistory. El Palacio, Vol. 62, Nos. 5-6, pp. 131-73. Santa Fe.

Wheat, Joe Ben
1955 Mogollon Culture prior to A.D. 1000. American Anthropologist, Vol. 57, No. 2, Part 3, (Memoir No. 82). Menasha.

Worman, Frederick C. V.
1959 1957 Archaeological Salvage Excavations at Los Alamos, New Mexico: a Preliminary Report. El Palacio, Vol. 66, No. 1, pp. 10-15. Santa Fe.

APPENDIX

IDENTIFICATION OF MAMMALIAN FAUNA

by

Arthur J. Jelinek

The animal bone from the Tesuque By-Pass Site comes from Area A; a majority of the specimens were recovered from the kiva.

In the descriptions which follow, "1" and "r" stand for left and right members, respectively. A summation of the specimens and the minimum number of individuals represented is given for each animal.

The identified animal bone from the kiva is listed in Table 1.

TABLE I

ANIMAL BONES RECOVERED FROM THE KIVA FILL, AREA A

Spec.	Level I	Level II	Level III	Level IV	Other	Total	Min. Ind.
Carnivora							
Dog *(Canis familiaris)*						5	1
Parietal-occipital	1						
Humerus (1), dist.					1		
Tibia (r)	1						
Phalanges	2						
Rodentia							
Cottontail rabbit							
(Sylvilagus sp.)							
prob. *audubonii*						16	4
Scapula (r)	1			1			
Humerus, dist.		1					
Ulna (r), prox.				1			
Radius (r)				1			
Pelvis (r)		1					
Pelvis (l)				1			
Femur (r)				2	2		
Tibia (r)	2			1			
Tibia (l)				2			
Jack rabbit *(Lepus californicus)*						18	2
Mandible (l)				1			
Scapula (r)				1			
Scapula (l)				1	1		
Humerus (r), prox.	1						
Humerus (r), dist.				1			
Radius (r)				1	1		
Radius (l)				1			
Pelvis (r)	1			1			
Pelvis (l)	1			1			
Tibia (r), dist.				1			
Tibia (l), prox.	1			1			
Calcaneum				1			
Astragalus				1			

Table 1 *continued*

Spec.	Level I	Level II	Level III	Level IV	Other	Total	Min. Ind.
White-throated wood rat *(Neotoma albigula)*						–	1
most of one individ.			x				
Wood rat *(Neotoma* sp.*)* prob. *albigula*						2	1
Pelvis (r)		1					
Femur (r)		1					
Pocket gopher, chestnut faced *(Cratogeomys castanops)*						2	1
Skull	1						
Pelvis	1						
Black tailed prairie dog *(Cynomys ludovicianus)*						6	2
Palate and frontal				1			
Ramus (r)		1					
Ulna (l)				1			
Radius (l)			1	1			
Pelvis					1		
Artiodactyla							
Elk *(Cervus,* sp.*)* prob. *merriami*						2	1
Femur (l), prox.	1						
Calcaneum (l)					1		
Bison *(Bison bison)*						1	1
Phalange (2nd)	1						
Mule deer *(Odocoileus* sp.), prob. *hemionus*						*89*	6
Frontal frag. w. antler base (r)	1						
Maxilla (r)		1					
First cervical vert.	2						
Misc. vertebrae	3			3			
Scapula (r)	1						
Scapula (l)		1					
Humerus (r), dist.	3	3					
Humerus (l), dist.	2						
Ulna (r), prox.					1		
Ulna (l), prox.	1	1	1		1		
Radius (r), prox.	2			1			
Radius (l), prox.	1						
Radius (l), dist.	2	1					
Pelvis (r), acetab.	1						
Pelvis (l), acetab.	2						
Femur (r), prox.	1						
Femur (l), prox.	3				1		
Femur (l), dist.	1						

Table 1 *continued*

Spec.	Level I	Level II	Level III	Level IV	Other	Total	Min. Ind.
Tibia (r), dist.	1			1			
Tibia (l), dist.	2			1			
Calcaneum (r)	2	1		1	1		
Calcaneum (l)	2				1		
Astragalus (r)	1						
Astralagus (l)	2			1	1		
Naviculo-cuboid (r)	1						
Naviculo-cuboid (l)	2						
Metatarsal (l), prox.	1						
Metatarsal, dist.	2			2	1		
Metacarpal (r), prox.	1						
Metacarpal, dist.					1		
Phalange (1st)	8	2		1			
Phalange (1st), prob. *Odocoileus*	3				1		
Phalange (2nd)	2	1					
Phalange (3rd)	1						
Pronghorn antelope *(Antilocapra americana)*						96	5
Frontal (r)	1						
Frontal (l)	1						
Orbit (l), lower rim	1						
Ramus (r)		1					
Ramus (l)	1	1					
Maxilla (r), frag.	1						
Basal (r), frag.	1						
Molar	1						
Auditory bulla (r)	1						
First cervical vert.	2						
Misc. vertebrae	4						
Scapula (r)	3						
Scapula (l)	2				1		
Humerus (r), dist.	2		1				
Humerus (l), dist.					1		
Ulna (r), prox.	3						
Ulna (l), prox.		1					
Radius (r), prox.	1	1					
Radius (r), dist.		1					
Radius (l), dist.		1			1		
Pelvis (r)					1		
Pelvis (l)*	4			1	1		
Femur (r), prox.	1						
Femur (r), dist.	1	1					
Femur (l), prox.	3				2		
Tibia (r), prox.	2	1					
Tibia (r), dist.	2						
Tibia (l), prox.	2				1		
Tibia (l), dist.	1			2			
Calcaneum (r)	2	3					
Calcaneum (l)	1	1					
Astragalus (r)	1						
Astragalus (l)	2						
Naviculo-cuboid (l)					1		
Metatarsal (r), prox.	1						
Metatarsal (l), prox.	1						
Metatarsal, dist.	3		1		1		
Metacarpal (r), prox.					1		

Table 1 *continued*

Spec.	Level I	Level II	Level III	Level IV	Other	Total	Min. Ind.
Metacarpal (l), prox.	1						
Metacarpal, dist.	3				1		
Phalange (1st)	1	2		2	2		
Phalange (2nd)	2						
Phalange (3rd)	2						

* Two fragments possibly from one individual

The identified animal bone from other features in Area A is listed below in Table 2.

TABLE 2
ANIMAL BONES RECOVERED FROM THE DWELLING AREA, AREA A

Spec.	T-3	T-7	T-4	Room 5 Rect. Part	Room 5 "D" Part	Rm.6	Rm.7
Rodentia							
Black tailed prairie dog *(Cynomys ludovicianus)*							
Ramus (l)				1			
Artiodactyla							
Domestic sheep *(Ovis aries)*							
Metacarpal (r) prox.					1		
Mule deer *(Odocoileus* sp.), prob. *hemionus*							
Maxilla (r)							1
Maxilla (l)							1
Ramus (r)		1					
Tibia (r), prox.			2				
Tibia (l), dist.			1				
Calcaneus (l)					1		
Metatarsal, dist.	1						
Metacarpal (l), prox.			1				
Pronghorn antelope *(Antilocapra americana)*							
Calcaneus (l)					1		
Metatarsal (r), prox.						1	

In addition to the above, two identified specimens of animal bone were recovered from the fill of Feature I in the Intermediate Area. They were a distal fragment from a humerus (r) of a mule deer and a proximal fragment from an ulna of a pronghorn antelope.

COMMENTS

In general, the identified animal bone specimens from Tesuque By-Pass Site are typical of the fauna found in the area during historic times. From the broken and shattered condition of the bones, it appears that all animals were used as food, with the possible exceptions of the pocket gopher (*Cratogeomys*), the wood rat (*Neotoma*), and the dog. Many of the bones show rodent-tooth marks. This may be explained by the presence of the wood rat. The pocket gopher, on the other hand, is primarily vegetarian and may have been eaten.

The most interesting forms, from the standpoint of present distribution, are the chestnut faced pocket gopher (*Cratogeomys castanops*), the black tailed prairie dog (*Cynomys ludovicianus*), and the bison (*Bison bison*). The two rodents are not found at present in the Rio Grande Valley north of the Albuquerque area. Although both occur in the normal range of an Upper Sonoran fauna, they are apparently more characteristic of a "Lower-Upper Sonoran" assemblage than of the "Upper Sonoran-Transitional" assemblage found in the area today (cf. Bailey, 1913). Their presence may indicate a somewhat warmer climate (including possibilities of both a longer growing season and greater aridity) than is typical of the Tesuque area at present.

The bison bone is from a very large individual. The absence of other bison material from the site suggests the possibility of a souvenir of an impressive animal brought back from the plains. Present knowledge indicates that bison were not native to the northern Rio Grande area at the time the Tesuque By-Pass Site was inhabited (Reed, 1955).

The one domestic sheep bone is more recent in appearance than the other material. Its association with the other faunal remains can probably be discounted on the basis of its shallow position in the site fill.

The absence of any bones other than the calcaneum and femur of the elk suggests that a single haunch had been carried back to the village from a hunting excursion in higher country.

Virtually all portions of deer and antelope are present and it is probably safe to assume that they were not hunted at any great distance from the village.

Analysis of the faunal remains indicates one rather puzzling factor: the absence of proximal extremities of humeri for the artiodactyls. There are thirteen distal ends and no proximals. Since the proximal portion of humeri does not appear to have been a favored raw material for tools, this may characterize local butchering techniques.

In conclusion, it may be noted that bone was not distributed uniformly through the fill of the kiva in Area A. The paucity of remains from level III suggests an early (level IV) and a late (levels I and II) use of the kiva for deposition of trash, separated by the time during which the level III fill accumulated. The amount of time involved is, at present, conjectural.

REFERENCES CITED

Bailey, V.
1913 Life Zones of New Mexico. North American Fauna, No. 35. U. S. Department of Agriculture. Washington.

Reed, E. K.
1955 Bison Beyond the Pecos. Texas Journal of Science, Vol. VII, No. 2, pp. 130-36. San Marcos.

PLATE I

Small sherds of painted pottery from Area A: *a-h*, Kwahe'e B/W; *i-k*, Red Mesa B/W; *l-m*, Gallup B/W; *n-o*, Chaco B/W; *p*, Santa Fe? B/W; *q*, Mancos? B/W; *r*, Wingate B/Red; *s-t*, unidentified B/W.

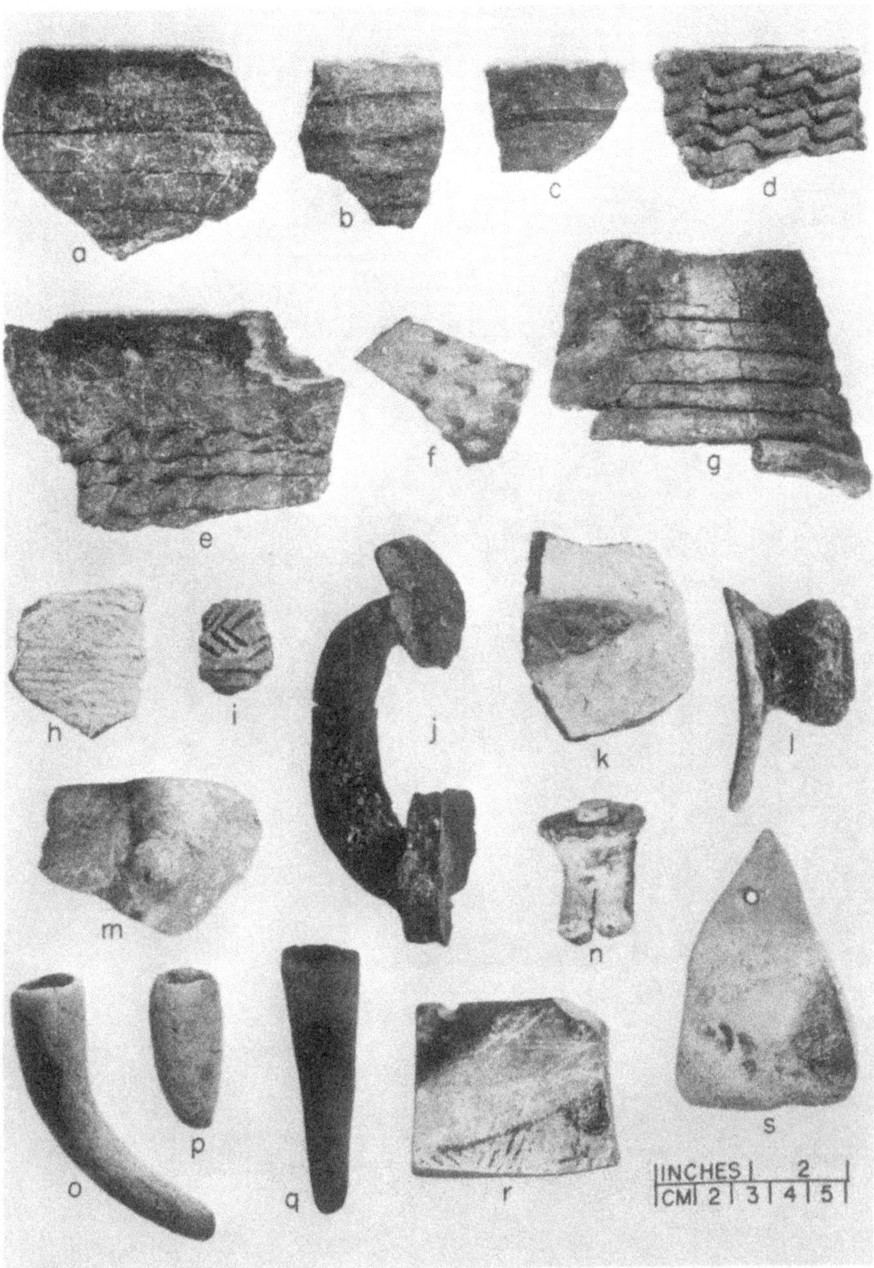

PLATE II

Unpainted pottery from Area A: *a-c*, neck-banded; *d-e*, corrugated; *f*, punctate; *g*, neck-ribbed; *h-i*, incised; *j-n*, handles and lugs; *o-q*, pipes; *r-s*, worked sherds.

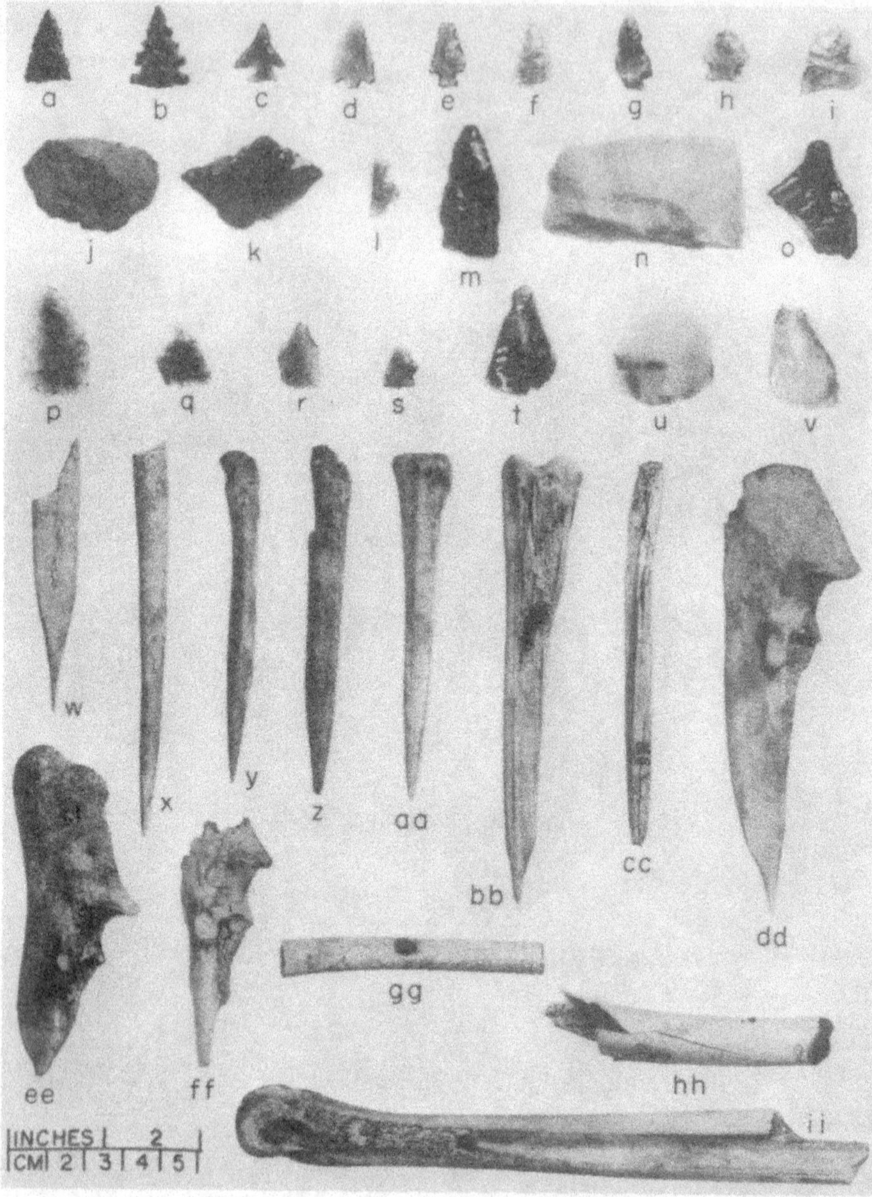

PLATE III

Small artifacts of stone, bone, and shell from Area A: *a-i*, points; *j-k*, chipped stone Group A; *l-o*, chipped stone Group B; *p-u*, chipped stone Group B'; *v*, shell artifact; *w-x*, awls Group F; *y-z*, awls Group C; *aa*, awl Group B; *bb*, *dd-ff*, awls Group A; *cc*, awl Group E; *gg-ii*, other worked bone.

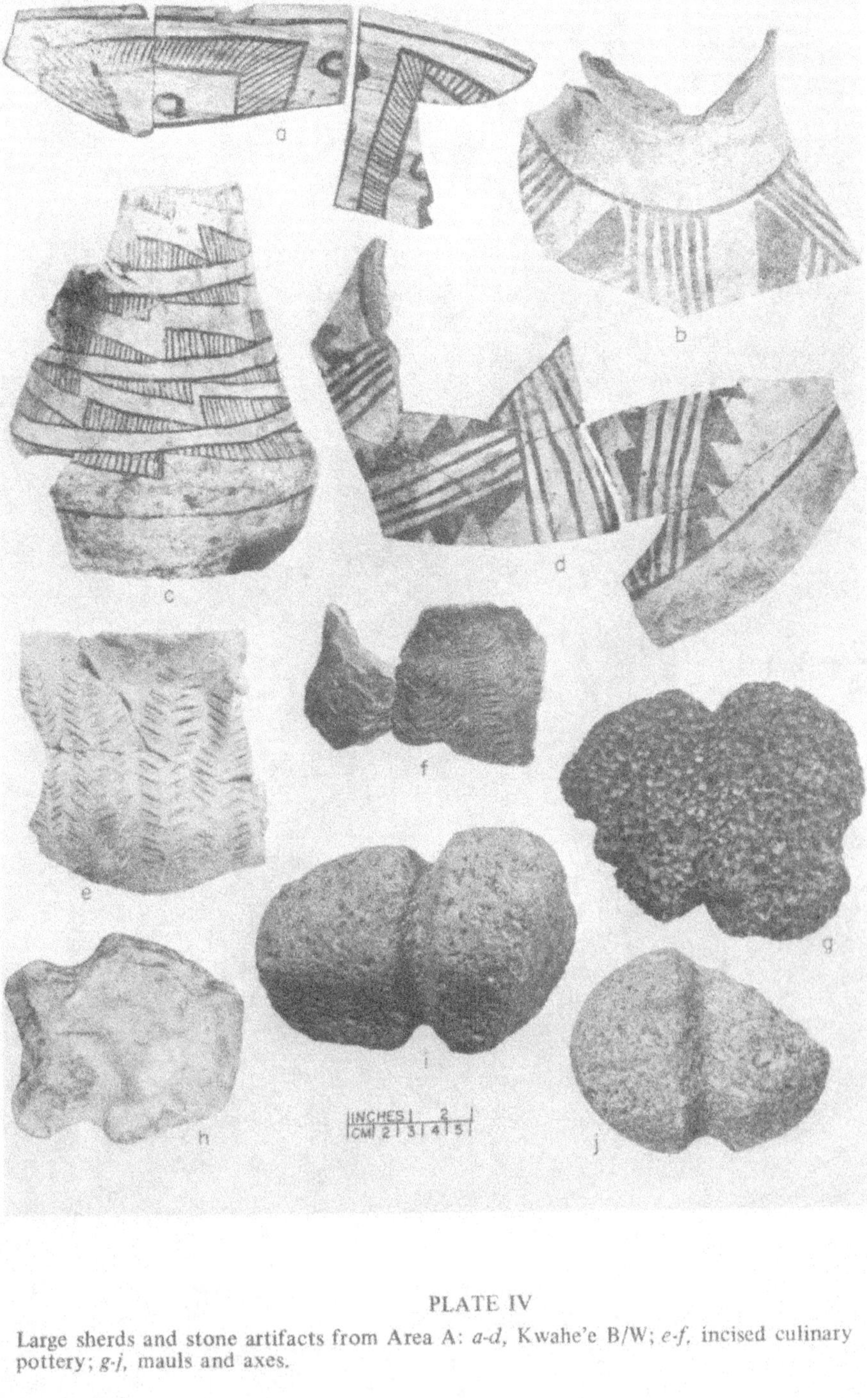

PLATE IV

Large sherds and stone artifacts from Area A: *a-d,* Kwahe'e B/W; *e-f,* incised culinary pottery; *g-j,* mauls and axes.

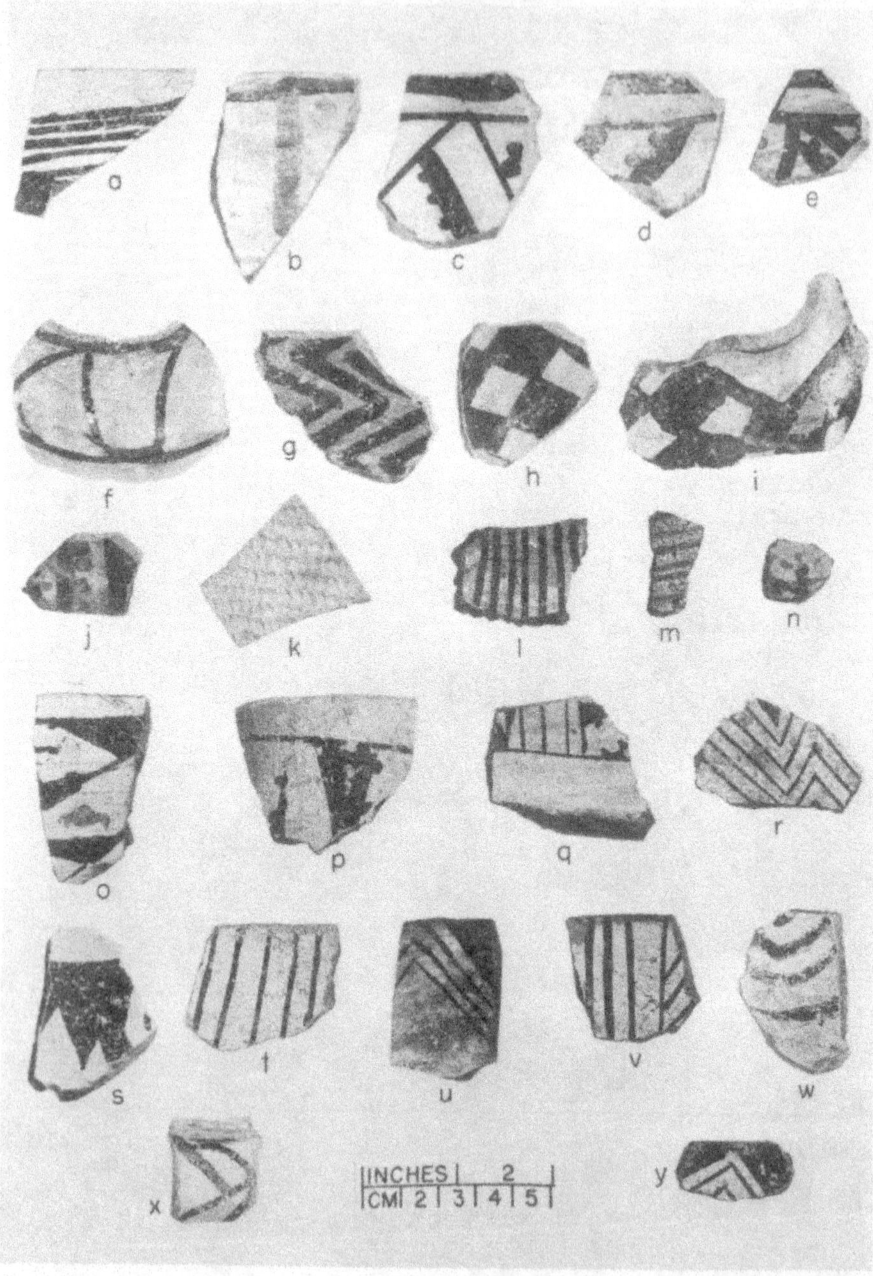

PLATE V

Painted pottery from Area B: *a-k*, Santa Fe B/W; *l-m*, Kwahe'e? B/W; *n*, Biscuit B?; *o-r*, Red Mesa B/W; *s-y*, unidentified B/W.

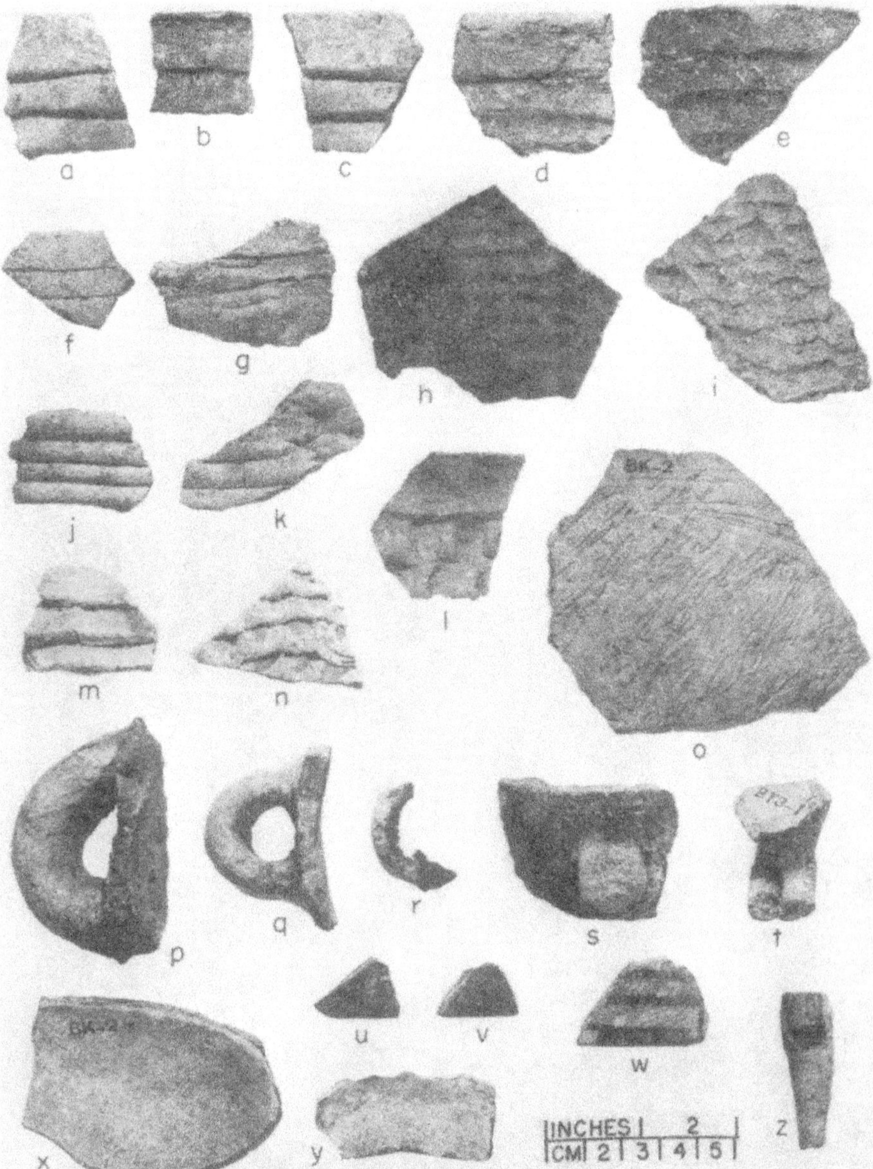

PLATE VI

Unpainted pottery from Area B: *a-g*, neck-banded; *h-i*, Tesuque smeared-indented; *j*, neck-ribbed; *k*, corrugated and ribbed; *l*, corrugated; *m*, Lino gray; *n*, corrugated and slipped; *o*, scored; *p-t*, handles and lugs; *u-y*, worked sherds; *z*, pipe.

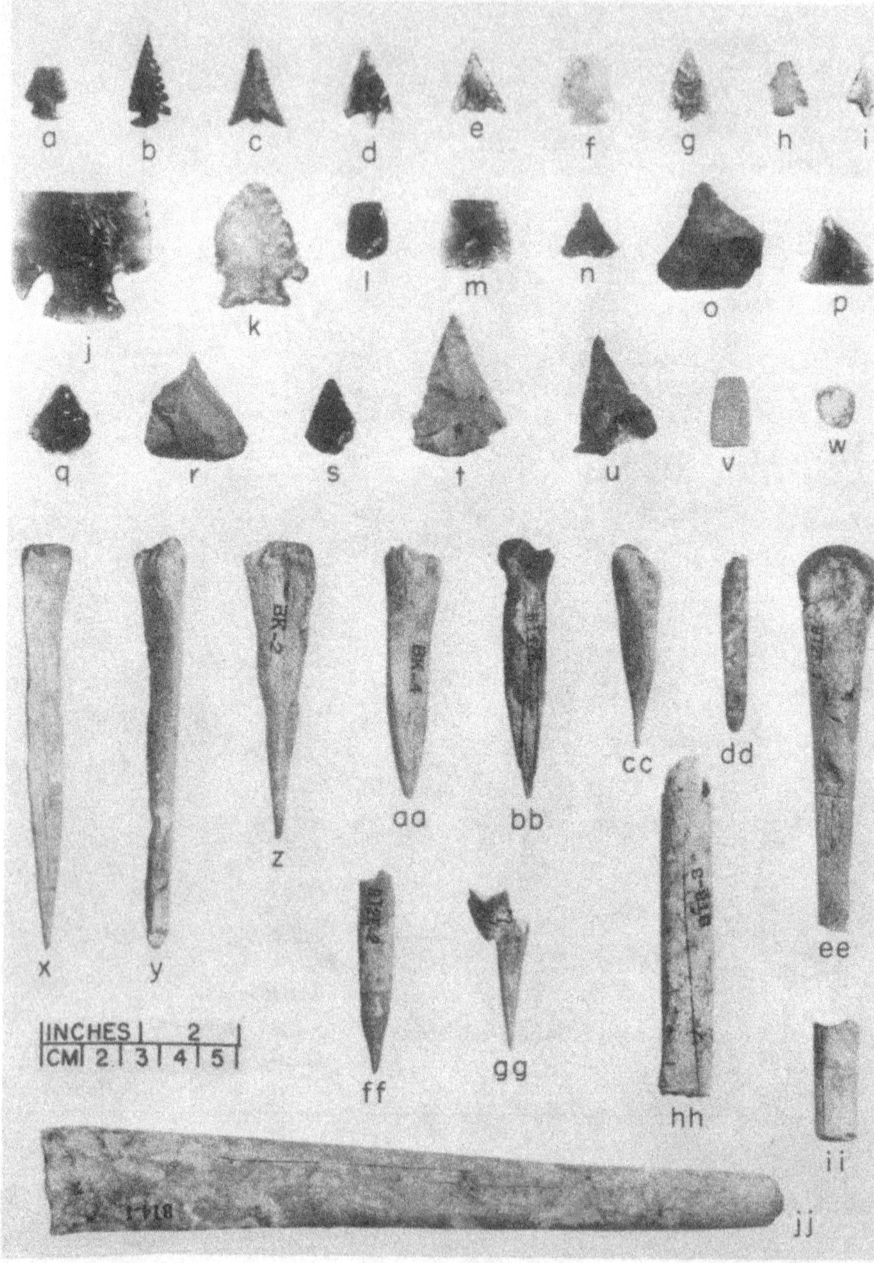

PLATE VII

Artifacts of stone, bone, and shell from Area B: *a-k*, points; *l-m*, chipped stone Group B; *n-u*, chipped stone Group B′; *v*, worked shell; *w*, worked turquoise; *x*, *z-bb*, *ee*, awls Group B; *y*, *cc*, awls Group C; *dd*, *ff-gg*, awls Group F; *hh-jj*, other worked bone.

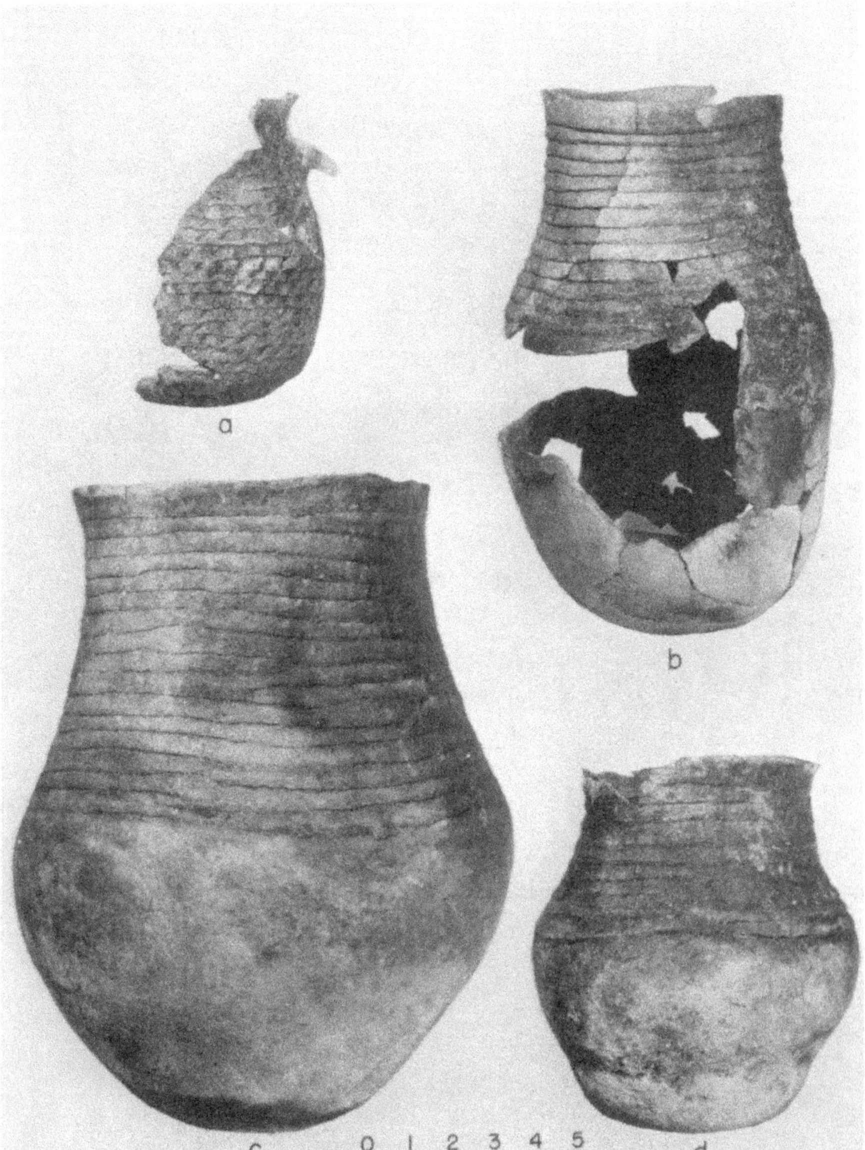

PLATE VIII

Complete and restored vessels from Area A and Area B: *a*, section of corrugated vessel, Area A; *b*, section of neck-banded vessel, Area B; *c-d*, neck-banded vessels, Area B.

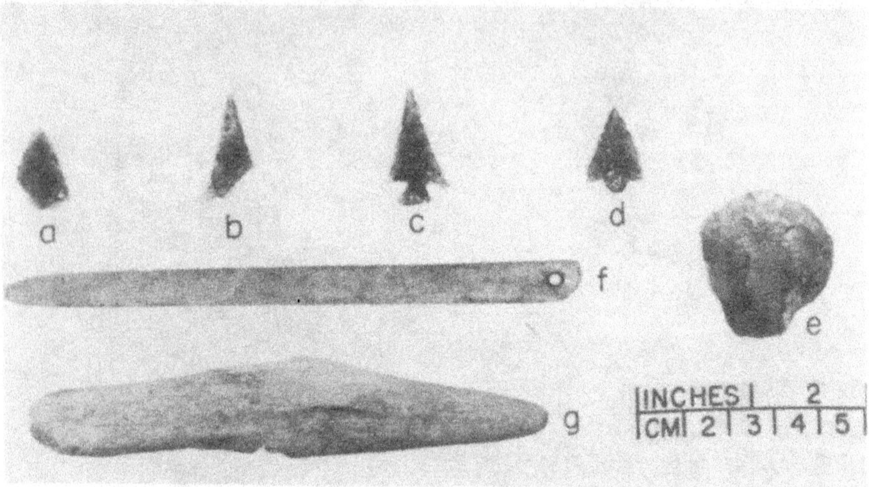

PLATE IX

Artifacts from the Intermediate Area: *a-e*, *g*, Feature I; *f*, Feature II.

a

b

PLATE X

Excavation photographs, Area A: *a,* The room-block, view NNW, scale is in Room 5; *b,* The kiva, view SSW, ventilator is at left.

a

b

PLATE XI

Excavation Photographs, Area B: *a,* Features A and B, view SW. The shovel, resting on the darker floor of Feature B, leans against the superimposed adobe wall. The lighter floor area is that of Feature A; *b,* The kiva, view NE. Ventilator, not shown, is to the right of the broken stone slab.

www.ingramcontent.com/pod-product-compliance
Lightning Source LLC
LaVergne TN
LVHW050022250826
846302LV00008B/56